International Educators' 2018 Hall Of Fame 25ᵗʰ Year Anniversary (1993-2018) Silver Jubilee

Biographies of the 2018 Inductees
Youth-on-the-Move, Inc.
International Educators' Hall of Fame

Patricia Adelekan, Ph.D.
Rick Gonzales

ADELEKAN PUBLISHING COMPANY
Garden Grove, California, USA

Copyright © 2018 by Patricia Adelekan, Ph.D.
2018 U.S.A. Edition
Printed in the United States of America

Library of Congress Cataloging -in-Publication
Adelekan, Patricia A. 1942

YOUTH-ON-THE-MOVE, INC. INTERNATIONAL EDUCATORS' HALL OF FAME 2018:

1. International Educators' Hall of Fame 2. Egyptian Educators 3. Educators' - International Educators' Hall of Fame 4. Educators' Hall of Fame - International 5. Afro-American Interview 6. Afro-American Educators. 7. Afro-American Hall of Famers - Education 8. Hall of Fame Educators. 9. Multi-cultural Educators' Hall of Fame 10. International Educators 11. Asian Educators 12. Taiwan Educators', Multicultural Role Models 13. Native American Educators. 14. International Educators 15. Humanitarian Educators 16. Hall of Fame Educators 17. Educators 18. Heroes 19. Pioneers 20. Trailblazers 21. Firsts in Education. 22. Orange County Educators. 23. Chapman University, International Educators' Hall of Fame, 24. Pioneer educators in Orange County 25. Intergenerational, youth and seniors in education 26. Educator role models, 27. Educator mentors

Library of Congress Card Number 97-651407
ISSN:10973656

ISBN: 978-0-9969355-6-2

All rights reserved. No part of this publication may be reproduced or transmitted in any form or by any means, electronic or mechanical, including photocopy, recording, or any information storage and retrieval system, without permission from the publisher.

Request of permission to make copies of any of the work should be mailed to:
Permission Department, Adelekan Publishing Company, Publisher,
P.O. Box 5983
Garden Grove, CA 92846, U.S. A.

To order:
Adelekan Publishing Company
P.O. Box 5983
Garden Grove, CA U.S.A.

714-628-9844
educatorshalloffame.org
IEHOF2015@gmail.com

What is a Hall of Fame?

"A Hall of Fame is a Museum with a Personality," says Buck Dawson of the document: International Swimming Hall of Fame. "Whereas an anthropological museum deals in the composite man, a Hall of Fame deals in specific men and women - personalities whose talent and achievement express biographically the dramatic episodes displayed in the Hall of Fame. Hence, it is a living museum, even though some of the honorees are deceased. It tells the story of measured accomplishment in the terms of the talented heroes and heroines who were the high achievers in the activity honored, be it music, theater, sports or education."

Patricia Adelekan, Ph.D., founder of the Youth-on-the-Move, Inc. Educators' Hall of Fame, 1993 in Sacramento, California, U.S.A., agrees that a Hall of Fame is a museum of living personalities and sometimes includes outstanding deceased educators. "Our Educators' Hall of Fame," she explains, "is where great souls are gathered for their accomplishments, unselfish giving and courage . We especially honor the retired educator and those who have served for at least twenty years in the educational arena. They also must have done more than just their duty."

And the term 'educator' is used in the broadcast sense of the word: all fields of study and all levels are honored – academic, science, medicine, tourism, childhood/nursery, religion, sports, law, aviation, the arts, etc.; pre-school educators through university professors. Research on Halls of Fame in the world reveals that this is the only one of its kind.

Any person may nominate a candidate. To be eligible for nominat ion, an educator must beretired and/or have served at least 20 years in the field and must have done more than the call of duty. Many are "Firsts," "Pioneers," "Trailblazers," "Survivors" and, they are all considered role models. After nominees submit the necessary documents, a rigorous selection process follows.

Finally, the selected Inductees are feted publicly and honored in a commemorative document International Educators' Hall of Fame: USA.

The Hall of Fame started as a local United States entity and became international in 1996. Overseas Celebrations took place in June 1997, February 1998, and April 1999. The YOMI Cultural Heritage Presentation Educators' Hall of Fame was established in Memphis, Tennessee, U.S.A in 1997; in the San Francisco Bay Area in 2000; for the first time in Orange County California, at the Chapman University, in 2013. We boast that in 2014, we opened the Educators' Museum and Learning Center in the city of Santa Ana, California, also in Orange County. The Hall of Fame educators are often the mentors, teachers, and story tellers for the youth, their families and others in the community who frequent our Museum and Learning Center.

Foreword

Spiritual understanding, universal knowledge, awareness, wisdom, and collaboration are the vital ingredients for survival in the world today and the next millennium. They are also characteristics of the humanitarian educators featured in the Youth-on-the-Move, Inc. International Educators' Hall of Fame.

As I review and look over the lives of these precious souls who span all corners of the earth, I am moved, shaken and awed by the rich lore of their creativity, diversity, quality, profound humanity, love, wisdom, knowledge and oneness of spirit. These are some great souls created, endowed, and placed on earth to give, to love, to dare, and to share.

These souls gathered by Him and placed in this International Educators' Hall of Fame are examples to others, as beacon lights, mentors and guides - How wonderful!!! Let us pay tribute to them all: pay 'tribute to whom tribute is due' and often overdue.

Thank you readers. Enjoy what the Spirit has brought together at the close of the 21st century in this and previous, commemorative, soul-inspiring historical document.

This year, in 2018, on our 25th year Silver Anniversary, we are proud to be celebrating in the city of Scarmento, California, where it all began. We invite you to read the stories of kindness as told by our 2018 Inductees in their biographical sketches in this book.

Sincerely,

Patricia Adelekan, Ph.D.
Founder, CEO

Table of Contents

What is a Hall of Fame?	i
Forward	ii
Title Page	iii
Copyright	iv
Table of Contents	v
Remembering Sandy Hook Teachers	vi
City of Anaheim Proclamtion	vii
Individual Inductees	viii
Dr. Florin John Ciuriuc	1
Holly S. Cooper	2
Edenausegboye Beulah Pearl Davis	3
Dr. Kevin Russell Gibbs	4
Raymond "Ray" Gutierrez, Jr.	5
Dr. Desmond Jolly	6
Aladrian Mack	7
Diane D. Chandler-Marshall	8
Jeraldine "Jerri" Lange	9
Doris I. Mangrum	10
Jacque Sherrill Tahuka-Nunez	11
Amagda Perez	12
Linda D. Rose	13
Dr. Elmer L. Towns	14
Harold Dean Trulear	15
Holly Viola Van Valkenburgh	16
A Word from a Scholar	17
International Inductees	18
Dr. Kaanchanapalli Govardhan Raju	19
Dr. Juan Carlos Ortiz	20
Posthumous Inductee	21
Julius Rosenwald	22
Family Inductee	23
The Rick Gonzales Sr. Family	24-25
Community Service	26
Mikhail Kishchenko	27
The Olivers; Bonnie Jean Pannell	28
The Roberts; Richard Nelson	29
Rick Warren; Alpha Bruton Family	30
Some Famous Hall of Famers	31
2018 Inductees	32
Hall of Fame Program	33
Yomi 33 Year Anniversary	34
Goals and purposes of Yomi Tutorial Program	35
Some Yomi Participants Through the Years	36
Mission Statement and Creed	37
The Mahender Adluri Family; Photos	38
The Oliver Family	39
The Adelekan Family	40
Testimonial Letter to Youth-on-the-Move	41
Where are they today? Oussama Deeb; Tamu Nolfo	42
Where are they today? Ricardo Gonzales; Rosalie Martinez	43
Edmond Family; Miguel Perez	44
Countries Represented 2018 Hall of Fame	45
Alumi Association Mission Statement	46
Legacy Museum and Learning Center	47
Board of Directors; Hall ofFame Committee 2018	48
Hall of Fame Book order form	49
Educators' Hall of Fame Nomination Form	50
Ads	51-61
About the Editor-in-Chief	62

Remembering the Teachers of Sandy Hook Elementary

Anne Marie Murphy

Dawn Lafferty Hochsprung

Rachel D'Avino

Lauren Rousseau

Mary Sherlach

Victoria Soto

*For the Hall of Famers listed in this attached letter. Remember the day.
Come and join us this year for our 25th Silver Jubilee Anniversary celebration.*

January 25, 2013
To Dr. Janet Robinson,

We, the members of the planning committee for the 2013 International Educators' Hall of Fame*, kindly request your assistance in forwarding our condolences to the families of the six educators who were slain in the Sandy Hook massacre.

As you will read, we honor outstanding humanitarian educators who have gone beyond the "call of duty" in serving others. Our hearts have been crushed at the thought of the sacrifices that these six Sandy Hook educators made on behalf of their students.

Herewith you will find letters to the families of the educator-victims. We have left each of the envelopes opened so that you may view them, also, if you wish. Your cooperation in this matter would be greatly appreciated.

Again, as Hall of Fame Educators, we ask that you accept our condolences at this most difficult time, and pass on the letters to the families.

Patricia Adelekan, Ph.D., founder and 2013 Committee Chair, and the 2013 planning committee members:

Al Wilson, Sacramento, CA
David Watkins, Ph.D., North Kansas City, Missouri
Lucia Birnbaum, Berkeley, CA
Dr. Loraine Boykin, Memphis, TN
Ida Dunson, Emeryville, CA
Carolyn Stokes, San Pablo, CA
John Favor, Tracy, CA
Pastor James Burnell, Tustin, CA
Reverend Dr. Adetokunbo Adelekan, Philadelphia, PA
Toni Colley-Perry, Sacramento, CA
Alpha Bruton, Chicago, Ill

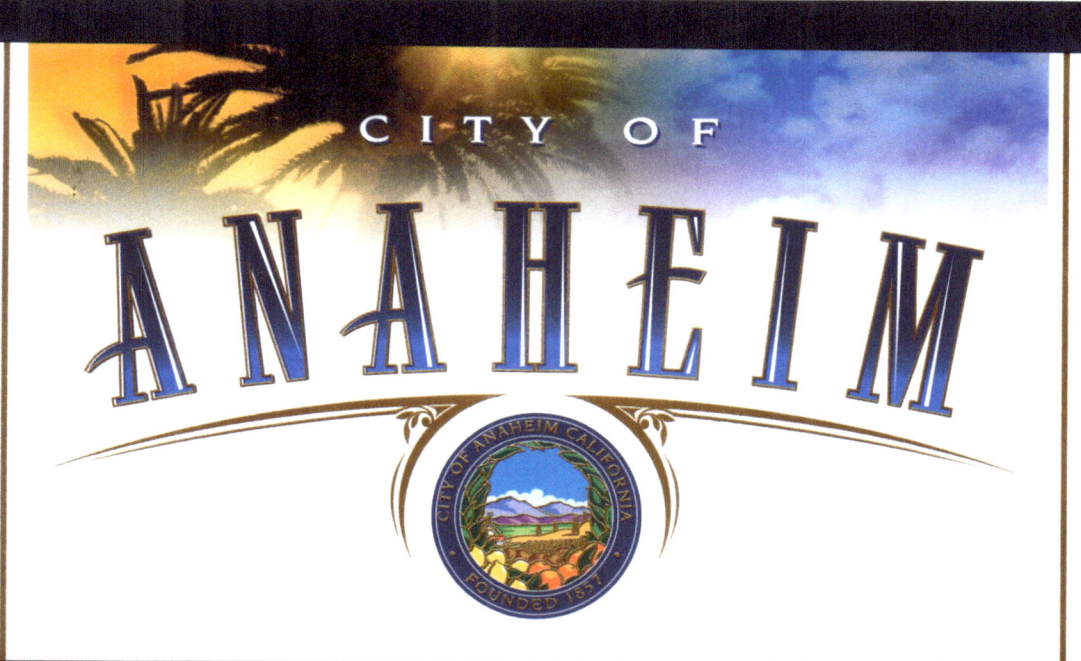

PROCLAMATION

Whereas, Youth-on-the-Move, Inc. was co-founded by Patricia Adelekan, Ph.D. in 1986 in Sacramento, California as a non-profit youth education organization to help youth succeed in life with the help of positive community role models, and The International Educators' Hall of Fame founded by Dr. Patricia Adelekan, in 1993 as the African American Educators Hall of Fame to seek and honor retired and 20+ years-of-service educators who have gone beyond the call of duty and served as beacons of light, mentors, and role models for youths and those who may benefit from added wisdom and motivation; and

Whereas, many of the Hall of Fame educators were founders, and pioneers in their fields of education, and were devoted and committed to excellence and positive results as their hallmark, these two groups became mutually supportive and effective collaborators, when in 1996 joined together, became multi-generational, multi-cultural, and international; and

Whereas, today, these two groups span over 35 countries, touching the lives of over 1,000,000 youths and boosting over 600 outstanding International Educator Hall of Famers; the youths have become compassionate mentees, mentors, role models, spiritual leaders, and responsible citizens of today; and

Whereas, today the purpose of the Youth-on-the-Move, Inc. International Educators' Hall of Fame and Youth Awards Ceremony is to seek for and give recognition to educators (and students) who have succeeded through dedication while facing numerous obstacles.

NOW BE IT HEARBY PROCLAIMED that the City of Anaheim recognizes, Saturday July 7, 2018 as Youth-on-the-Move, Inc. Day in the City of Anaheim for its 33rd Year Anniversary, and the Silver JUBILEE of the International Educators' Hall of Fame.

ISSUED: This 7th Day of July 2018

Tom Tait
Mayor

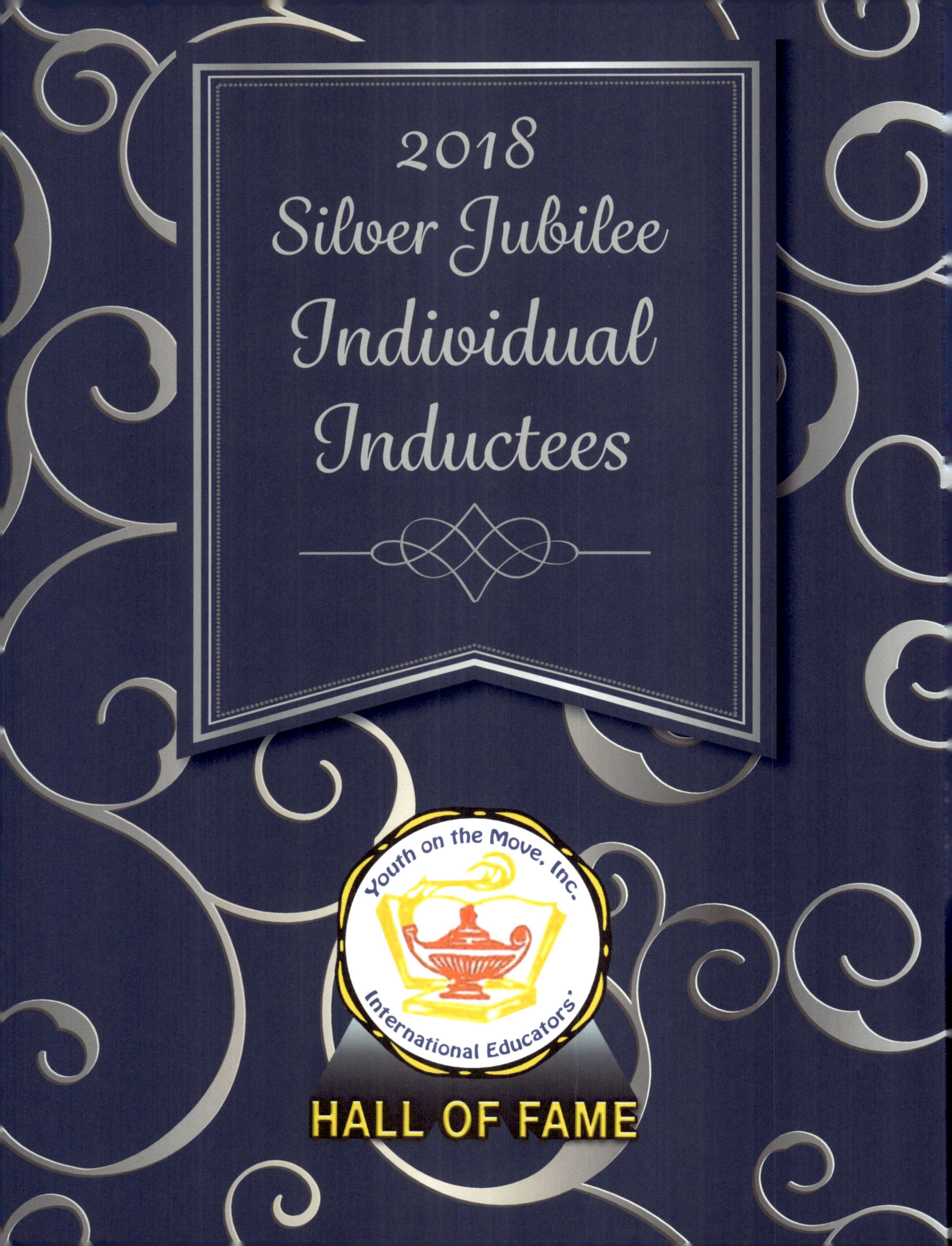

Dr. Florin John Ciuriuc

Born: Romania, April 14, 1969

Dr. Florin John Ciuric received his early education in Romania (the former Communist Socialist Republic of Romania), where he was born. He came from a poor immigrant family; his dad was a former Soviet Intelligence officer who was wounded in 1943 by a German sniper in the Check Republic and was never allowed to returned to his home in the Ukraine. His mother was not educated; the family had a hard life, he says. Florin was the 4th of six children. On June 10, 1986, at the young age of 16, Florin escaped from Romania, without having a chance to say "good-bye" to his parents or brothers and sisters.

"I just disappeared – walking for five days and four nights all the way to Belgrade, Yugoslavia where I turned myself in to the United Nations," he recounts. A year later, on June 12th 1987 (at age 17), he was put into a Yugoslavian political prison without knowing what would happen to him. During his stay in prison, and not knowing any English, he heard through the prison walls, President Reagan (who had travelled to Berlin to promote peace) say, "Mr. Gorbachev Tear Down this Wall." Florin says that "from that moment on, I was given a chance to be alive and to pursue my dream of coming to America. Soon after, in 1988, Florin arrived in America.

Once in America, Florin learned English and pursued education in criminal and civil law, crime prevention, criminal defense investigations, immigration and citizenship. He has been training and teaching in these fields for over 28 years. "I got involved in educating the youth and parents about the danger of gangs, drugs and criminal activities." Because of his travels and interest in helping others, Florin is currently writing an inspirational book containing 100 stories from 100 individuals called *America, My Home and Yours*. He says, one question he asks every person he writes about – including himself is "Are We Calling America Our Home? And Why?

Dr. Ciuriuc earned his two law degrees in International and U.S. law and is constantly busy volunteering helping thousands of Slavic immigrants adjust to America; he teaches them how to become knowledgeable and reliable citizens. For his services and kind heart, he has received myriad awards and titles: "The Slavic-American Leader," by the U.S. and foreign governments; and as an effective Community Educator by many.

In 2016 Florin become a candidate to the Belarus Republic for Hon. Consul in California and was approved by the Belarus government in 2018. In 2017, the Republic of Malawi, in Africa recognized him as the Good Will Ambassador in America.

His Advice to youth: "Please love Our Mighty God; love your parents; love your family; stay in school, get your education; and go after your dreams... Finally, be a good citizen, be a good patriot, and love America."

His favorite quotation: "Don't ask what the country can do for you. Ask what you can do for your country," by President J.F. Kennedy, 1960.

Florin has a close-knit family: a wife and six children. "We have many stories," he says. He often thinks about his family left behind in Romania.

Holly S. Cooper

Born: San Antonio, Texas, March 16, 1971

Holly attended elementary in Lubbock and high school in Houston. She completed her Bachelor's Degree from UC San Diego in 1993 and her J.D. in 1998 at UC Davis, School of Law. For the past twenty years, Holly has taught law students about immigration rights in Arizona and in California. She has trained over 200 college students and law students to become immigration defense lawyers.

As a young girl in rural Texas, Holly went to school where she was one of the only non-Latino children. She learned Spanish from the other children and was welcomed into their community from a place of trust and love. Learning Spanish is a lifetime gift that has enabled her to access a critical understanding of her clients, friends and community members that other whites do not have.

Holly endured a traumatic experience as a child that, at times, impacts her ability to represent abused children. However, her child clients themselves always inspire her to continue the fight when she shares with them her own experiences. They have a secret shared solidarity and they motivate each other.

Holly is the Co-director of the UC Davis Immigration Law Clinic where she teaches law students how to defend immigrant rights. She has been training and teaching students for 20 years and still teaches at UC Davis School of Law. She has a full-time course load dedicated to hands-on teaching (clinical education). Holly's awards include the Mexican American Concilio Community Award, the Legal Services for Children's Outstanding Community Partner Award, the Yolo County Multi-Cultural Community Council Award, the Woman of the Year for District 04 (selected by Assemblymember Aguiar-Curry) and the Carol Weiss King Award from the National Lawyers Guild (teaching award).

An outstanding accomplishment was when Holly and her students, working with the ACLU, won a class action injunction against immigration authorities for wrongfully classifying Latino youths as gang members. The case forced ICE to give each child the right to contest his/her classification as a gang member in a hearing. Due to the lawsuit, judges have found 90% of the Latino immigrant youth were misclassified as gang members. Holly has published extensively about immigration rights and injustices.

Her advice to youth: If you took all the hours you wasted staring at your phone and created art, music, wrote a story, hiked through nature or cultivated our communities, you would be unstoppable.

One of her favorite quotations: "Wherever they might be, they always remember that the past was a lie, that memory has no return, that every spring gone by could never be recovered, and that the wildest and most tenacious love was an ephemeral truth in the end."

-Gabriel Garcia Marquez, *One Hundred Years of Solitude*

Edenausegboye Beulah Pearl Davis, mpa

Born: Port Gibson, Mississippi, July 17, 1957

Ms. Davis received her early education in the State of Mississippi where she was born. She, with her family, soon moved to California where she earned an AA Degree with Honors, at Sacramento City College and a B.S. degree in Organization Behavior and a Master's in Public Administration, both from the University of San Francisco.

Ms. Davis was highly influenced by her parents and both sets of grandparents, and, especially by her biology teacher, Dr. Joan Dunbar who chose Ms. Davis as the student Dunbar felt would reach "fame and fortune." This pronouncement was a surprise to her, declares Ms. Davis. And such prediction fostered a solid foundation she would need to succeed in life despite the challenges she would have.

Ms. Davis says she has struggled with poverty and racism. She quotes Mahatma Gandhi: "Poverty is the worst form of violence." And racism she says opened her eyes about the injustices that exist because of it. As a brilliant, high school honors student, Ms. Davis was never called to the counselor's office for any financial support, suggestions and/or recommendations on future college, university, vocational trades opportunities. So, when she and her other "A"-student friends went themselves to the counselor's office for advice, they were immediately informed that they should find work at a factory.

But because of "God and praying families, those honor students forged ahead, and today they are all successful educators, lawyers, military retired officers, etc.," states Ms. Davis.

Ms. Davis considers her being hired by the Sacramento Women's Civic Improvement Club (WCIC)/Playmate Child Development Center, Head Start Programs provided the blessed opportunity for her to use her God-given skills (teaching, organizing, and management) and values (compassion, caring and love) to the maximum. She hired, trained and guided staff who would teach preschoolers to develop a solid foundation in academics and soft skills that would last a lifetime.

While serving at WCIC, Ms. Davis has a tremendous impact on all people (adults and children and families) that experience her compassion and care. Indeed, for over forty years, she has made a difference in the Oak Park Community and in the lives of thousands. For her grand accomplishments in leading, managing, administering, and teaching these skills, she has received many outstanding awards: a Sacramento Employment and Training Agency (SETA) Governing Board Resolution, 12/16/2011; California Black Chamber of Commerce Leadership Award; and many more.

Her Advice to youth: "know and love yourselves and study your history. "When one knows thyself, one will know their God-gifted talent and use that talent by praying, practicing, developing, nurturing their God given token, which will help you out of poverty. Remember, especially, to help someone else and/or as many as you are able to.

Her favorite quote is from Mahatma Gandhi, "You must be the change you wish to see in the world." Ms. Davis' family is where her life begins and LOVE never ends. All her family have been supportive and encouraging to her along her journey.

Dr. Kevin Russell Gibbs

Born: Youngstown, Ohio, December 14, 1960

Kevin received his early education in Youngstown, Ohio and received training at the University of Maryland. In Okinawa, Japan and Embry Riddle Aeronautical University at Travis AFB, he completed his general education toward his earned degree for the Community College of the Air Force. He also attended Sacramento Bible College and various community Colleges. In December 21, 1995 he earned a Bachelor of Theology, in 1999 he received a Master's degree in Biblical Studies and in 2011 received a Doctorate of Theology from Sacramento Bible College and Theological Seminary.

He has been in the field of both formal and informal education for over 33 years. He was the CEO and President for 3 years of Ecclesia University – a Christian Bible College that offered degrees from a Bachelor to the Doctorate level. The curriculum ranged from the undergraduate degree program doctoral degree.

Dr. Gibbs was reared by his grandparents who encouraged him to finish school and to pursue the calling of God to educate all who would listen and allow him to help them to pursue their passion and gift from God. He was the first college graduate from his family.

A turning point in life for Kevin was when he enlisted in the military – "It was a frontier in my life that prepared me for the rest of my life on how to confront and handle the challenges I would face in the world and in my future career," he says.

Kevin says one of the biggest obstacles in life was "himself. "I got in my own way at times; my faith in God and prayer got me through the difficult times." Another difficult time was when he went through a divorce – "the fear and challenges were enormous, and sometimes endless; however again my faith in God and His Love toward me gave me the courage to persevere, adapt and overcome."

Kevin has received various awards in life: the Chaplain Leadership' Award given by the Chaplaincy when stationed at Suwon AB in Korea; and the Leadership and Community Involvement Certificate by Mather Veterans Village Leadership Staff. At Mather, Dr. Gibbs is the first Chaplain for the Mather Veterans Village, located in Rancho Cordova, California.

Dr. Gibbs taught history, as a substitute teacher, at the Montessori School in Okinawa, Japan for 3 years, and has coached a youth basketball team for five years while stationed in Ramstein AB, Germany.

Today, in 2018, Dr. Gibbs owns a Business Partner Administration (BPA) company through the Department of Motor Vehicles (DMV). Through this business he provides services like those of AAA, license plates, stickers, renewal of registration and title services.

His advice to youth: "It takes hard work, dedication and believing in what you are doing and that success is not determined by money and fame. And, "No one can make you feel inferior with your consent." By Eleanor Roosevelt.

Raymond "Ray" Gutierrez, Jr.

Born: Woodland, California, December 10, 1932

Ray attended Beamer Elementary, graduated Woodland High School, then attended and graduated from CSU, Chico with a BA and a General Secondary Credential in 1960. Ray then furthered his education at CSU, Sacramento earning his MA in Education followed by his Administrative Credential in 1975. He earned his Community College Credential and his Community College Supervisor Credential in 1980.

The first turning point that impacted Ray was when he was picking cotton in Visalia. He made up his mind that this was not going to be the way of life for him. The second turning point was when his Baseball coach encouraged him to go to college.

The first obstacle Ray encountered was a language barrier. When he started school he spoke and understood only Spanish. Fortunately for Ray, he had some teachers who understood his situation and spent a lot of one-on-one time helping him.

The second major obstacle was being the first Latino educator in his community. Ray had to prove that he could succeed with the challenges in front of him. His wife and family were always there when he needed encouragement.

Ray has been honored and received awards from the Sacramento Mexican American Hall of Fame, the Sac-Joaquin Section Hall of Fame, the Woodland Community College (WCC) Founders Award, the Latino Community Council Aguila Unity Award and the WCC Chicana/o Studies Award.

Ray was the first young Latino from Woodland to go away to college and then come back home to teach for the next 55 years.

He tells the story of when his family came back from Mexico and he started school for the first time. He entered first grade at the age of eight speaking only Spanish. He was struck across the palms of his hands with a ruler because he had not followed her instructions which were given in English.

Ray Gutierrez was not only the first Latino teacher, coach, Counselor and Administrator in the Woodland Joint Unified School District but also the first at the Woodland Center Yuba College (now Woodland Community College). His advice to youth: "I would tell them to set realistic goals, develop a plan to meet your goals, and use all resources available."

His favorite quote is: "Si Se Puede (Yes, I can do it)."

Ray's wife, Barbara, is a retired educator. They will celebrate their 60th wedding anniversary in August. Their son, Steve, is a UCD graduate. Their two daughters, Brenda and Ann, are both successful in the business world. One grandson, Cody, graduated from the University of South Alabama and is now serving in the Navy preparing to become a Navy Seal. Granddaughter, Ariana, is going into the 5th grade. Ray emphasizes that his family keeps him going

Dr. Desmond Jolly

Born: Jamaica, May 17, 1939

Desmond attended Green Island Elementary School, Ruseas Secondary in Lucea, Cornwall College in Montego Bay, all in Jamaica. He earned a Bachelor of Science in Economics from Utah State University in 1965, and both a Master's and PhD. in Economics in 1973 at the University of Oregon.

Desmond was an educator for fifty-two years. His mother instilled in her children a hunger for education. She led by example. At age 19, Desmond tried to become a farmer and entrepreneur. It was not a burning success. He was always a good student and was encouraged to use his brain to do something else. As a Teaching Assistant at the University of Oregon, he discovered that he was an effective teacher.

His first years at Utah State University were challenging due to cultural shock and cultural isolation. He chose to focus on his work and dream of more pleasant times and the end of his sojourn in Utah. He had a couple of professors who liked and supported him. Desmond was the first black economist in the history of the Department of Agricultural Economics at the University of California at Davis in 1971. You can imagine the time and the place and the challenges he faced as a pioneer. He gives credit to his wife and children for moral support. A few professors supported him and gave him the opportunity to show what he could do as an educator. Fortunately, his students responded positively.

As far as community involvement, Desmond helped develop "Embracing Diversity, Creating Community-A Multicultural Curriculum Resource Guide, Grades K-12 in 1992. He also developed the Multicultural Leadership Institute in the Meadowview area of Sacramento in 1993. This was a first for the Sacramento area as well as Desmond's first in such an endeavor.

Awards include the Yolo County Concilio Recognition Award in 2006 and the City of Davis Human Relations Commission Thong Hy Hyung for Community Education in 1993. Desmond received the Outstanding Black Agricultural Award from the Agricultural Economic Association in 2005 and the California Farm Conference Individual Achievement Award in 2004. He also co-developed the first General Education Undergraduate Course in the UC system in Agricultural Biotechnology, Ethics and Public Policy.

His advice to youth: "Patronize your neighborhood or school library. Wherever I was, I made the library my second home. Also get exercise and fresh air."

One of my favorite quotations comes by way of my father. "The heights of great men reached and kept were not attained by sudden flight. But they, while their companions slept, were toiling upwards through the night."

Desmond's wife is Julia Annette Jolly. She has been a professor and an Administrator at Sacramento City College for 30 years. They have two children. Tony is a pediatrician. Their daughter, Katherine, is a professor of music at Indiana University.

Aladrian Mack

Born: Houston, Texas, November 2, 1941

Aladrian attended Clawson Elementary School, Woodrow Wilson Junior High and Oakland Technical High School in Oakland, California. She attended Merritt College and transferred to San Francisco State University where she earned a BA degree in 1971. She completed her Master's at Sonoma State University in 1998. Aladrian has been in the field of Early Childhood Education for 45 years. Her parents were her first major influences and supporters. Because of her interest in children, her parents found a preschool program where she could volunteer. After that experience, she knew that she wanted to attend college and learn everything about the world of the early learner.

Her community involvement includes 10 years as a member of the Board of Directors of the Peregrine Project and Peregrine School. This work included identifying cultural biases and how they affect teaching practices, and, then working with teachers and staff in building an anti-bias school environment. Aladrian worked with the UC Davis Women's Cardiovascular Medicine Program to create the "National Faith-Based and National Community Cardiovascular Disease Prevention Programs for High-Risk Women." As a member of the Sacramento Chapter of the Links, Inc., Aladrian served for twenty-five years on The Links Achievers Program that honored outstanding African American male high school seniors. In that role, she created workshops on finance, health, etiquette and project management. Over the years these young men have become highly successful college students and men in their chosen professions.

During fifteen years of her work as the Manager of Educational Services, Sacramento County Head Start Program, she worked with Head Start teaching staff across the county to create and sustain a curriculum that reflected current child development principles and responded to the diverse cultures of the children and their families. Through this training, the teachers learned to have respectful conversations with parents that determined favorite family rituals and cultural items to be shared in the classroom. Over the years, teacher practices led to the Sacramento County's teachers being recognized as teachers of distinction by the National Office of Head Start.

Aladrian was selected by the California Office of Teacher Credentialing to serve as a member of the review team evaluating the quality of the credentialing program within the California State University system. She also conducted an in-depth review and assisted the Alaska Family Services Head Start Program, Fairbanks, Alaska in reaching Federal Compliance Standards.

Aladrian has received a Commendation for establishing the National Head Start Education Coordinators Network, Department of Health and Human Services, Washington, D.C. She received from the Davis City Council a Community Service Award.

Her advice to youth: "Whoever said you have to go it alone, never played a team sport. We all need others to help us reach our goals in life. Ask others to participate in your dream."

One of her favorite quotes: "There is nothing so satisfying, so defining of our character than GIVING OUR ALL To a difficult task." By Barack Obama

Diane D. Chandler-Marshall

Born: New York City, New York, April 11, 1956

Ms. Diane Chandler-Marshall's work includes extensive experience with both local and national-level government, public and private organizations, and non-profit arts agencies. Her career in the arts spans 30 years as an arts administrator and advocate.

Ms. Chandler-Marshall's active role in the arts and cultural planning is the foundation for her belief in the arts as a vital component of all communities and the important aspects they contribute to creative, intellectual, and financial stability of the communities they serve.

Currently, she is the Education Director for the Jazz Institute of Chicago. In this role she serves as Administrator of the Jazz Institute's Jazz Links programs, which includes, Artist Residences, The Jazz Links Student Council and Teachers Advisory Council, the Jazz Ambassadors Summer Camp, the Straight Ahead Jazz Camp for Instructors, The Kiewit-Wang Mentorship Award and the "Jazzin' Up Chicago Public Schools Professional Staff Development Workshop for Chicago Public School Music Instructors.

Prior to joining the Jazz Institute Team, Ms. Chandler-Marshall served in the Central Office of Chicago Public Schools as the Director of the Bureau of Cultural Arts.

The Bureau's mission served to advocate for academic, cultural and social development through the arts. The Bureau operated a range of city-wide programs in dance, drama, music and visual arts.

Under Ms. Chandler-Marshall's leadership, in 2002 the Bureau began a significant three-year research project to determine the impact of arts education on academic achievement, entitled "Improving Academic Achievement through the Arts" (IAAA).

In 2005, she co-authored The Arts: Keystones to Learning, a publication documenting the 26 schools in this initiative. Ms. Chandler-Marshall believes that arts education is a critical foundation for a child's comprehensive development, and that a creative learning environment is essential for the academic achievement and success of all children.

In 1999, Ms. Chandler-Marshall was awarded the Music of the Heart Education Award by the National Association for the Recording Arts and Sciences, Inc. for her outstanding contributions to music and arts education.

Ms. Chandler-Marshall graduated from Columbia College with a Bachelor of Arts, majoring in Arts and Entertainment Management with a special emphasis in Non-profit Arts Management. She received a Master of Science in Marketing Communications from Roosevelt University in 1994, graduating with Honors.

Jeraldine "Jerri" Lange

Born: Oakland, California, January 3, 1925

Jeraldine Lange received her early education in Berkeley California and she attended Laney College, in Oakland, California. She has been in the field of education for over 40 years. She was a professor of Broadcast Communications Arts at San Francisco State University, and she also lectured graduate students in Communication at Stanford University.

From 1969 to 1979, she worked for as a journalist, public speaker, and television talk show host – all in a quest to educate the masses. She hosted community-minded television programs on KEMO; KBHK; KGO; and KQED where she interviewed megastars like Shirley MacLaine; Sammy Davis, Jr.; Rock Hudson; heads of states and governments, historians, activist, and politicians.

A turning point in Jerri's life was believing that her knowledge and experiences were valuable enough to share with the world. From this realization Jerri says "This is how I began seriously writing, and that writing turned into several published books and papers, and many lectures."

Another turning point was her traveling around the world and working as a special correspondent in Africa for the San Francisco Chronicle. "I enjoyed meeting and interviewing some the most fascinating people and learning about different cultures." She says one her most exciting moments was when she was granted an interview with Professor Arnold Toynbee, an historian and member of the Royal Institute of International Studies in London.

Jerri has received many awards for her outstanding work: The Outstanding Broadcaster of the Year; In the Spirit Award; Artists Embassy International – Literary Award and many others.

Her involvement in the community has been enormous: she was the first woman president of the Board of the American Lung Association of San Francisco; served on the boards of the Oakland Symphony, the Food Bank of Contra Cost and Solano Counties, and KQED Television. She was the first Black woman to serve as Personal Secretary under San Francisco Mayor, John F. Shelley in 1966. She is also her family's representative for the Michael F. Lange Foundation – created for honor her late son, Michael – to continue his vision and work in the community.

Her advice to youth: "Stay around people who will lift your spirits, and stimulate our mind, and love learning. Take it upon yourselves to learn as much as possible about the things that interest you and about how you can make a difference in your communities and the world."

One of her favorite quotations: "We need more light about each other. Light creates understanding, understanding creates love, love creates patience and patience creates unity" by Malcolm X

Jerri was married to Theodore "Ted" Lange, Jr. and they had three children. Her oldest son Theodore "Ted" Lange III became famous for his role as Isaac Washington on the TV series LOVE BOAT, and as Junior on another TV series That's My Mama. Her middle son, Michael, passed away in 2015; he left a legacy of love and commitment for his community. He also played Malcom X hundreds of times in various productions. Her youngest son, James is a businessman in San Francisco Bay Area.

Doris I. Mangrum

Born: Savannah, Georgia, July 7, 1942

Doris I. Mangrum received her primary and secondary education in Mississippi. She then attended Bakersfield College in Bakersfield, CA where she earned an AA Degree. She also earned a BS Degree in Music Education in 1973, and did graduate studies in Savannah Georgia and San Rafael, CA. She has an AA degree in Early Childhood Education and many units towards an MA degree in Human Development.

Doris has spent over 35 years in the field of education. When she was growing up, her parents, Eugene and Ardelma Isaac were her greatest inspiration. Doris says they grew up poor, but went on to have successful careers as college professors.

A turning point in her life involved when Doris volunteered in a correctional facility and met families of the incarcerated. Prior to that experience, she says she didn't understand the collateral impact of incarceration on those left behind at home and in the neighborhood. "Such an experience influenced my journey to work to bring attention to the impact of imprisonment on families," explains Doris.

In early 2000s, Doris says she was invited to appear on a television talk show. "After the interview, the host suggested that I go into broadcast work," says Doris. "Shortly thereafter, I began hosting and executive-producing radio shows." She says she later segued into television and has been working in the broadcast arena since that encouraging suggestion. "I have used the media to expand the reach of my work," she says.

Doris works with the incarcerated and their families. The mindset of most of society is to maltreat persons who have collided with the criminal justice system. Her role to shift that paradigm and to include family in program planning to improve reentry outcomes is challenging but encouraging. Doris is active in many communities. She hosts and executive-produces, Education in Our Community and Stop the Madness: Practical Ways to influence the Incarceration Crisis.

She developed reading circles and libraries at churches which continue today. She co-designed transformative mentoring program for children of incarcerated parents. In 1987, in Bakersfield, California, she facilitated the opening of a preschool from idea to implementation. In 2011, she created a documentary called STAINS: Changing Lives After Incarceration which premiered at Tribeca Cinemas in New York.

Recently, the City of Oakland, the California State Senate, and Congress recognized her for her veterans' support and criminal justice reform. KPFA 94.1 FM named her "First" Community Hero for work in criminal justice.

Her advice to youth: "Do . . . **Do Not Try.**" The only way the word try should enter into your vocabulary is to "try . . . harder," " try . . . longer," "try . . . until you succeed."

One of her favorite quotes: "We must recognize people by their humanity and not by our perception of their issues. By Doris I. Mangrum.

Doris has been happily married for 40 years. She has three children: two boys and one girl. Doris says each has very successful careers and that she is very proud of them.

Jacque Sherrill Tahuka-Nunez, B.A., B.S.

Born: San Pedro, California, December 15, 1952

Jacque received her BA degree at the University of Southern California (USC) in 1980 in Speech Communications; and her BS degree from Hope University, in Business Management, in 1993.

Jacque grew up with hardworking parents in Orange County; she always knew she liked people. She loved meeting customers at her family's business, and her goal for the future was to be a union cashier. During those early days, Jacque often played school. She loved to motivate and guide others.

One day, her high school drama teacher, Maryina Herde, said to her, "You are gifted and talented, and you can go to college." These 10 words changed Jacque's life forever: she gained and grew her self-confidence, planned to go to college, and went.

Who could have imagined that fifty years later, she would receive the honor of being named the "State Native American Educator"?

USC Professor Dr. Leo Buscalia also greatly encouraged her: "VOLUNTEER. Give of yourself at least thirty hours this semester, he said to the class. Jacque took his advice and volunteerd at the Foundation for the Junior Blind, where she volunteered 200 hours. Next, she wrote and directed a play. And one day, her professor addressed her class of 400 students: "This young lady exhibits the kind of loving, heartfelt dedication required of a great teacher." His powerful, positive words reinforced her desire to become a teacher.

Jacque developed her speaking skills on the USC Forensics Team and was named 1980 Speaker of the Year. Her most memorable gold medal, however, was First Place at the National Speech Tournament.

Jacque says Mother Teresa and Dr. Martin Luther King, Jr. greatly inspired her. "Darkness cannot drive out darkness; only light can do that. Hate cannot drive out hate; only love can do that." Dr. Martin Luther King, Jr.

Jacque has been an educator for over forty years; she has received myriad awards including the Mayor Bradley Service Award, and Teaching Making a Difference Award, to mention a few.

For seventeen years, she taught in her hometown, San Juan Capistrano, where she lived with her husband and children. She felt called to share the story of her own Native American Juaneño/ Acjachemen Tribe .At first, her success as a storyteller was not embraced by her own tribe, but her faith in the Creator and knowledge of her gifts opened doors and won hearts.

Jacque has many firsts: she was the first Native American to write and direct a play viewed by 100,000 students over twenty-five years; she created the first educational program at Mission San Juan Capistrano; she developed the first Native camp in Orange County; she was the first Acjachemen to broadcast her storytelling on a national native network, and she was the first Acjachemen to film segments of a children's show called Abalone Dreams.

Jacque's advice to youth: "Pay attention to yourself. Discover what you love to do, and always find ways to do it. Respect yourself and your neighbor. Celebrate diversity."

Amagda Perez, Esq.

Born: Lakeport, California, November 7, 1966

Amagda graduated from Kelseyville High School in CA. She had a double major in Spanish and Chicano/a Studies at UC Davis and graduated with Honors in 1988. She earned her law degree from UC Davis, School of Law in 1991. Amagda has been a professor at UC Davis for 24 years.

Her mother and sister, both educators, and her father have influenced her success as an educator. As role models they taught her that teachers have the greatest impact when you teach a student and not a subject. One major obstacle early in her teaching career was just being accepted as a professor at law school.

In highlighting the successes of her students and her pedagogy in bridging the achievement gap of law students-of-color, she slowly began to earn the respect and acceptance of some of her colleagues. Professor Cruz Reynoso has been an incredible mentor and advisor who has shared his words of wisdom generously to help her overcome the challenges in academia. But her family have been her greatest motivators. They keep her going when "times are tough."

Her community awards include the State of CA Woman of the Year Award in 2018 by Assemblymember Aguiar-Curry, 4th District; Diversity and Principles of Community Team Achievement Award in 2015; the Pilar Andrade Award of Excellence in Advocacy presented by the Mexican American Concilio of Yolo County in 201; and the UC Davis School of Law Distinguished Teaching Award in 2010.

Amagda's most innovative accomplishment is coupling a law school clinical program with a non-profit legal service organization to provide students with a practical, client-centered lawyering experience working in and serving rural communities. Another accomplishment has been to speak to the hearts of students who have doubted they belonged in law school; she help them find their voice as advocates for their clients.

She has published widely about immigrant rights and injustices. She had the privilege of directing the CRLA Foundation and co-directing the UC Davis Immigration Law Clinic that has assisted more than 40,000 lawful permanent residents to become US citizens, approximately 2500 childhood arrivals to secure Deferred Action for Childhood Arrivals (DACA) status, and provided outreach and information to thousands of mixed-status families to inform them of their rights and help protect them from notario fraud and other abuses.

Her advice to youth: "Believe in yourself, don't ever give up on your dreams or let anyone tell you that you cannot accomplish what you want; stay true to who you are; draw strength from your family when the going gets tough, and above all, love what you do."

One of her favorite quotations: "Few things can help an individual more than to place responsibility on him, and to let him know that you trust him" by Booker T. Washington. She says, "because it is how I teach my students, they often tell me that the clinic experience was the most powerful learning tool, and that my confidence in them helped them successfully represent their clients.

Linda D. Rose, Ed.D.

Born: Birmingham, Alabama, June 5

Dr. Linda D. Rose earned her high school education in California; an Associate of Arts degree in Liberal Arts from West Los Angeles Community College; a BA degree in Interdisciplinary Studies and an M.A. degree in English, both from the California State University, Dominguez Hills (CSUDH), and a doctorate degree (Ed. D.) in Education Leadership from the University of California, Los Angeles (UCLA).

She has spent over 24 years in the education arena. Dr. Rose's mentors, college professors and supervisors during her first five year of teaching in a community college greatly encouraged herto be a success. Entering and beginning college, and earning a doctorate degree were turning points in Dr. Rosa's life. AT both stages, she was encouraged, inspired and motivated to be a leader and to give back to others who were entrusted to her.

As Dr. Rose progressed in life, she encountered a few challenges: 1) child care; 2) being an adult female returning to school; and 3) limited financial, physical, and moral support for returning adults on a college campus. She was able to survive these challenges by reading biographies of Professors and community members who made changes in the world by overcoming, persevering and championing their own causes, dreams, and challenges.

Dr. Rose is actively involved in various communities around the globe; she is a regular presenter, keynote speaker, and workshop facilitator; she especially enjoys participating in a Leadership Skills Seminar that focuses on issues facing women in community college administration. She has received hundreds of awards, such as Cerritos College Outstanding Administrator Award; Cerritos College Outstanding Faculty Award for the Liberal Arts Division; Who's Who among America's Teachers, Fifth Edition; National Institute for Staff and Organizational Development Teaching Excellence Award, and Businesswoman of the Year by the National Hispanic Business Women Association.

Two of her most outstanding accomplishments are (1) becoming a college president and (2) rearing two successful adult engineers who are dedicated and persistent and who follow their hearts in terms of what they want to do, and that she admires their intelligence, sensitivity and achievements.

She advises youth to know and understand that education is a powerful tool of transformation and that they will always have a choice. One of her favorite quotations is "Feel the fear and do it anyway." By Dr. Susan Jeffers.

Today, in 2018 Dr. Rose serves on the board of the Santa Ana Chamber of Commerce and the Santa Ana Workforce Development Board, and their Economic Development Board and Youth Council, respectively.

Dr. Elmer L. Towns, Dean, Min.

Born: Savannah, Georgia, October 21, 1932

Dr. Elmer L. Towns received his early education in the State of Georgia. For higher education, he attended

1. Northwestern College, Minneapolis, MN, where he received his B.A. Degree;

2. Southern Methodist University, in Dallas, Texas, where he received his MA in Philosophy of Education;

3. Dallas Theological Seminary, Dallas, Texas, where he received the Master of Theology (THM);

4. Garrett Theological Seminary, Evanston, Il, where he received the MRE in 1958; and finally,

5. Fuller Theological Seminary, Pasadena, CA, where he received his Doctor of Ministry in 1982.

Dr. Towns has been in the field of religious education for over 60 years. As Professor, Dean, etc.

He has taught and administers at Midwest Bible College, St. Louis, MO; Winnipeg Bible College, Manitoba, Canada; Liberty University, Lynchburg, VA. – to mention a few places.

As one would expect, there were obstacles along the way: The first major obstacle to his education was finances; thus he worked many part-time jobs and pastored part-time at various churches to help make ends meet. The second obstacle was finishing his education at accredited colleges. "I was refused admission to several colleges because my previous degrees were non-accredited. When they later received accreditation, I was given entrance."

His greatest accomplishments include the receiving of the Gold Medallion from Christian Booksellers Association and Christian Publishers Association for writing the best-selling book, *The Names of the Holy Spirit.* "No one in the history of Christianity has written a book or articles on the names of the Holy Spirit."

Dr. Elmer Towns and Jerry Falwell are well-known as the co-founders of Liberty University in Lynchburg, VA; which has become the largest private Christian college/university in the US.

He is further known for years as "Mr. Sunday School," has written over 200 books and is a LEGEND in Christian Education.

He has travelled to 19 countries to view the work of Christianity from "indigenous eyes." The results of this travel experience appear in an article: "Growth of Christianity in the Global South" (below the equator), and the Orient Crescent, i.e. China and South Korea.

His advice to youth: "First, measure your success in relationship to setting goals with your talents and abilities, and then reach and surpass those goals. If you try to reach goals set by other people and achieve successes they've achieved, you will probably end up being defeated. That failure will not lead you to success, but rather will defeat the very nature of success you're striving to achieve.

Two favorite quotes: (1) "Leadership is influence." By John Maxwell and (2) "You can't achieve what you don't conceive."

Dr. Towns lost his wife of 60 years in 2013; he has three grown professional children of whom he is proud.

Harold Dean Trulear, Ph.D

Born: Philadelphia, Pennsylvania, October 4, 1954

Dr. Trulear received his early education in Philadelphia, Pennsylvania; he earned his M.S. degree (Phi Beta Kappa graduate) from Morehouse College in 1975; and both his Master's and Doctor of Philosophy degrees from Drew University, in Madison, New Jersey, in 1979 and 1983 respectively.

Rev. Dr. Harold Dean "Doc" (as he is often called) Trulear is an ordained American Baptist minister and serves as Associate Professor of Applied Theology at Howard University School of Divinity since 2003, where he is also immediate past president of the Gamma of DC chapter of Phi Beta Kappa. He currently teaches Prophetic Ministry, Ethics and Politics; Ministry and Criminal Justice; and Church and Communities Studies.

Further, he is also the Director of the Healing Communities Prison Ministry and the Prisoner Reentry Project of the Philadelphia Leadership Foundation designed by the Annie E. Casey Foundation. Healing Communities USA is an organization that trains and supports congregations in their work with individuals and families impacted by crime and mass incarceration. It has been implemented in over 25 sites nationally, in partnership with such organizations as the Progressive National Baptist Convention; The General Board of Church and Society of the United Methodist Church; and the D-Free Ministry..

He is one of America's foremost "Change Agent" Ministers – a theological educator and social researcher. His achievements include research on youth, young adults, religion and public policy and his important monographs: Faith-Based Initiatives with High Risk Youth; The African American Church and Welfare Reform, and George Kelsey: Unsung Hero." He is co-editor of the book Ministry and Prisoners and Families: The Way Forward (Judson Press 2011), and author of over 100 articles, book chapters, essays and published sermons.

In 2014, Dr. Trulear was named as one of "14 Faith Leaders to Watch" by the Center for American Progress. He also served as a member of the Executive Session on Community Corrections at the Kennedy School of Government at Harvard University from 2013-16.

"Docs" advice to youth: "You were created to love. You were created to be loved. So many of us look for love in all the wrong places. Gangs make us feel like we have a family. Drugs and alcohol make us feel like we fit in. But, only a love that can't be taken away from you will sustain you in the difficult times that are sure to come. An education is good, but wisdom is better. You can be smart and not wise. Be wise with whom you surround yourself – for they will be primary determinants of your success."

Dr. Trulear is married to Vickie Lynette Butler and they have three children: Harold Butler, Jared Morgan, and Frances Elizabeth. His family has always been very supportive in whatever direction God sends him.

Holly Viola Van Valkenburgh

Born: New York City, New York, November 22, 1936

Holly Van Valkenburgh received her early education in New York City; New Jersey; and Boulder, Colorado. In 1957, she earned her BA degree from the University of Colorado with a major in Education; in 1965, she earned her MLIS (Masters in Library Science) from the University of Denver; and in 1987, her MA in computers in Education. Holly has been in the field of education for over 50 years.

When she was growing up Holly says she was her own inspiration to succeed in the field of education: "I was interested in what I did as a student library assistant at the University, and went on to earn my way as a professional," she says.

Two turning points in Holly's life: (1) "being told as an elementary school teacher that I did not need a Master's Degree to be a school librarian," and (2) "earning a Master's Degree in computers in education which trained me to install and use computer programs." Both of these experiences provided Holly with the necessary talents to teach library staff in Nevada libraries in many different ways.

Holly says her major obstacle on her way to success "was people I worked with who objected to my talents being better than theirs."

Being creative, curious, and diligent Holly became involved in various community activities: she was named "Woman of the Year" by the Nevada Women's History Project (NWHP); and one of her outstanding accomplishments was "earning my second MA from Distance Education which meant instructors were sent to the Indian Reservation monthly to teach us (trainees) how to utilize and teach computers to high school students."

Today, Holly is retired and does significant travel within and outside the United States; she belongs to three book clubs; participates in Organizations as a regular and board member: the American Association of University (AAUW); Friendship Force; NWHP; and the C5= Carson City Classic Cinema Club.

She advises youth to "Get as much EDUCATION as possible and plan to return for more (education) in future years to keep "up to date." One of her favorite quotations: "The Price of Sanity is UP."

Holly has three children (one daughter and two sons), four grandchildren, and five great grandsons. "My daughter, especially has been a wonderful influence on my life with, and treatment of, my children as they were growing up. When she was 16 I (Holly) knew she would not live to be 18 because I was going to clobber her myself; she is now MY BEST FRIEND."

A Word from a Scholar

Minister Adetokunbo Adelekan, Ph.D.

Princeton Theological Seminary
Princeton, N.J. USA, 1993

Since the dawn of history, the human spirit has been engaged in a never-ending, oft-eluding quest for social enrichment and communal betterment. In every generation there are a precious few who rise above the tide of popular opinion and assail the storms of egoism, social blindness and collective inertia that threaten the fabric of our common humanity. These 'great unselfish souls' possess the rare capacity to trace the sign of the moment and to discern the opportunities and possibilities of the human soul for their particular age.

Endowed with the prophet's imagination, the visionary's drive and the school teacher's persistence, they diligently attend to the work of the human situation, sometimes under the menacing eye of an unforgiving public, sometimes in the back room of some forgotten building, and oftentimes abandoned in the desolate desert of fate and destiny, but always free to tap into that inner source that compels them to face adversity-come what may. Such are many of the individuals featured in this book!

The human spirit is most free when enmeshed within the urgent vitalities of time and place, on behalf of some life-transcending and world-engaging purpose, actively pursuing the enrichment and betterment of all. Patricia Adelekan, my mother and teacher, is one of those spirits whose creative and compassion vocational 'impulse' transports us ever closer to the actualization of our dignity and worth as human beings. Her personal ethic embodies the olympian heights and expansive breath of a deeper and more profound reality than the one that we now face. As my mother has often said "Our capacity to strive and to fulfill our potential reflects our appreciation of God's Grace." This compendium — one that is distinguished by the commitment, character and concern of some of the most noble spirits of this generation — is an extension of her life dedication to the ethics of personal development, family uplift and communal concern en route to social transformation and human betterment. We thank God for such a masterful mother and teacher.

This book that you are now reading is a testament of hope for coming generations, for it bears witness to the rich legacy of moral courage, scholarly excellence and spiritual wisdom. The lives of the personages presented in this book are characterized by the indelible stamp of engaging and loving wisdom. Love is the one distinct quality that blends this variegated pantheon of educators into a unifying whole.

The lives of these individuals disclose the rich lore of creativity that permeates our common humanity. Their life-work and teachings signify the ability of the intellect and imagination to embrace moral centredness, intellectual excellence and critical social engagement. Their voices collectively speak to the pertinent issues of our social life, the sense of our collective worth and the power of the Almighty. Through these educators, we hear, we listen, we see, we follow, we walk across the pastures of destiny, to become the light of the world. Hail to the educators featured in this book!

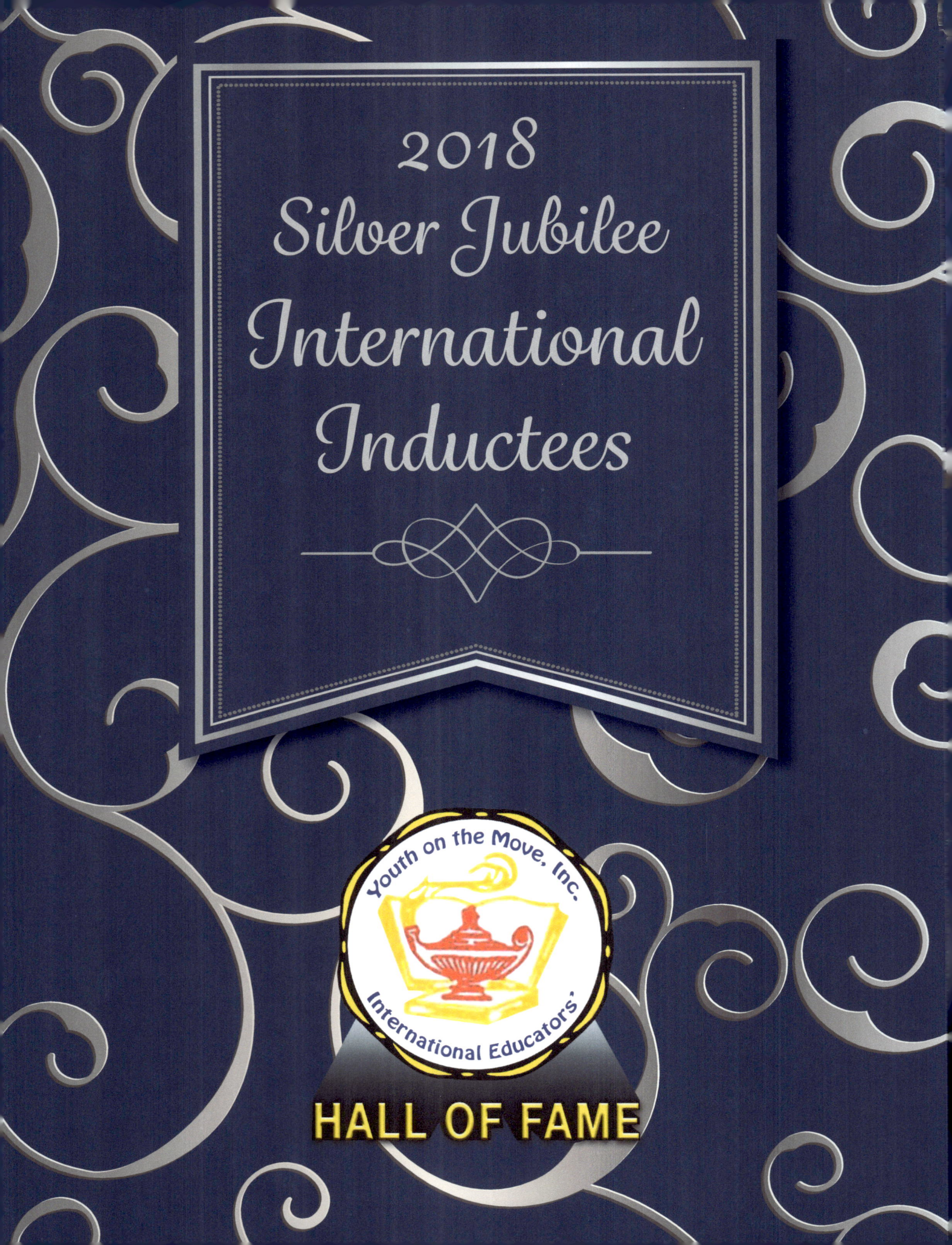

Dr. Kaanchanapalli Govardhan Raju

Born: Julapalli (Karimnagar), India, September 11, 1960

Dr. Raju Kaanchanapalli received all of his education in India: his early education K-Bachelor's degree in Karimnager and his M.A. and Ph.D. degrees from Hyderabad. He has spent over 29 years in the field of education.

While growing up, Raju's parents, both educators, influenced him to be a success in the field of education. Also, he was inspired and influenced by Dr. C Narayana Reddy, an Gyana Peet Awardee. Dr. Kaanchanapalli is also gifted in poetry writing and literature.

During his early life, Dr. Kaanchanapalli, encountered a few obstacles which prepared him for "tougher times" of the future. For example, when he was 12 years old, one evening, he missed a road home, and there was no public transportation nearby that would take him home. So, he walked to find public transportation to go home. This search for transportation lasted the whole night, and, at 6:00 a.m., he finally found the necessary transportation. From this night-long search, he says "that was my first hurdle that I overcame, and it had a great impact on me: it made me learn to overcome troubles."

Another obstacle occurred when Dr. Kaanchanapalli was pursuing his Bachelor's degree: the night before an examination, he observed a terrible accident which upset him greatly. As a result, he feared that he would not do well in the exam the following morning. But, the encouragement and motivation from his uncle and friends helped him to succeed well on the exam.

Dr. Kaanchanapalli stays involved in his community. In honor of his late mother, who died in 2003, he presents each year the "Lalitha" Award (named after her) to the best students. He provides sick students with medication to improve their health. Since 2015, he donates 15000 Rupees every year to poor children. He has published numerous poetry books to inspire his students at every level.

Among his most outstanding accomplishments, Dr. Kaanchanapalli Govardhan Raju wrote and published a book of poetry encouraging students not to commit suicide. He has greatly inspired society through his Telugu poetry books: Cheda Bavi [a 1994 - collection of poems]; Tandlata [2011 - A Long poem]; Kala Inka Migile Undi [2015 - a collection of poems]; Bhava Manjari [a poetry book]; and others.

He completed his M.Phil. in 1990, a Long Poem in English and Telugu Literature, and pursued his Ph.D. on The Evolution of Romantic Genres In English and Telugu Literature. He is also proud of the fact that he held conferences in 31 cities on behalf of Telangana Jagruthi to inspire students and citizens to establish a good civil society.

Today, Dr. Kaanchanapalli travels throughout India and the world conducting public conferences, writing poetry, working as an editor to publish books, reading novels, and performing various community services.

His advice to youth: "Have clear goals, be sincere, and work hard. It always pays off." A favorite quotation: "There is no defeat until you stop trying."

Dr. Kaanchanapalli is married with two married daughters. They always encourage and respect him, and his humanitarian lessons and contributions.

Dr. Juan Carlos Ortiz

Born: Buenos Aires Argentina, July 8th, 1934

Dr. Juan Carlos Ortiz is Pastor Emeritus of the Crystal Cathedral in Garden Grove, California.

He was born in Buenos Aires, Argentina on July 8, 1934, in a very devoted Christian Family, and was active in the church since childhood.

He graduated in the Assemblies of God "Instituto Bíblico Río de la Plata" school of theology in 1954 and ordained as a Minister in 1956 in the Christian Assemblies of Argentina. At present he is a minister in the Reformed Church of America.

Dr. Ortiz has founded six churches and was pastor of the largest evangelical church of those days in Buenos Aires from 1966-1978.

His vast experience in discipleship, small groups and leadership spirituality has taken him to conventions, congresses, universities, seminaries and churches in more than sixty countries in five Continents. He has received an honorary degree from the California Graduate School of Theology.

He has been a professor at the Instituto Bíblico Río de la Plata in Argentina, at the International School of preaching in the Crystal Cathedral in California and at present he is the president and professor at the School of Theology of Shepherd University in Los Angeles.

He also continues to accept some of the many invitations from around the world and from the U.S. to teach at conferences and seminaries of different denominations.

For five years, Dr. Ortiz produced the television series, La Hora de Poder (The Hour of Power) which was aired in twelve countries in Latin America. He has also produced two radio series one in Argentina and the other in Los Angeles.

His books are world renown: DISCIPLESHIP, CALL TO DISCIPLESHIP, THIS GOSPEL WILL BE PREACHED, THE CRY OF THE HUMAN HEART, LIVING WITH JESUS TODAY AND GOD IS CLOSER THAN YOU THINK.

Some of these have been translated into most European and Asiatic languages.

From December 2008 to August 31 2009, as the Senior Pastor of the Crystal Cathedral resigned, Dr. Ortiz was call to be the Interim Senior Pastor or that Church.

Dr. Ortiz and Martha Palau were married in 1961 and have four children, six grandchildren, two great grandchildren and live in Tustin, California.

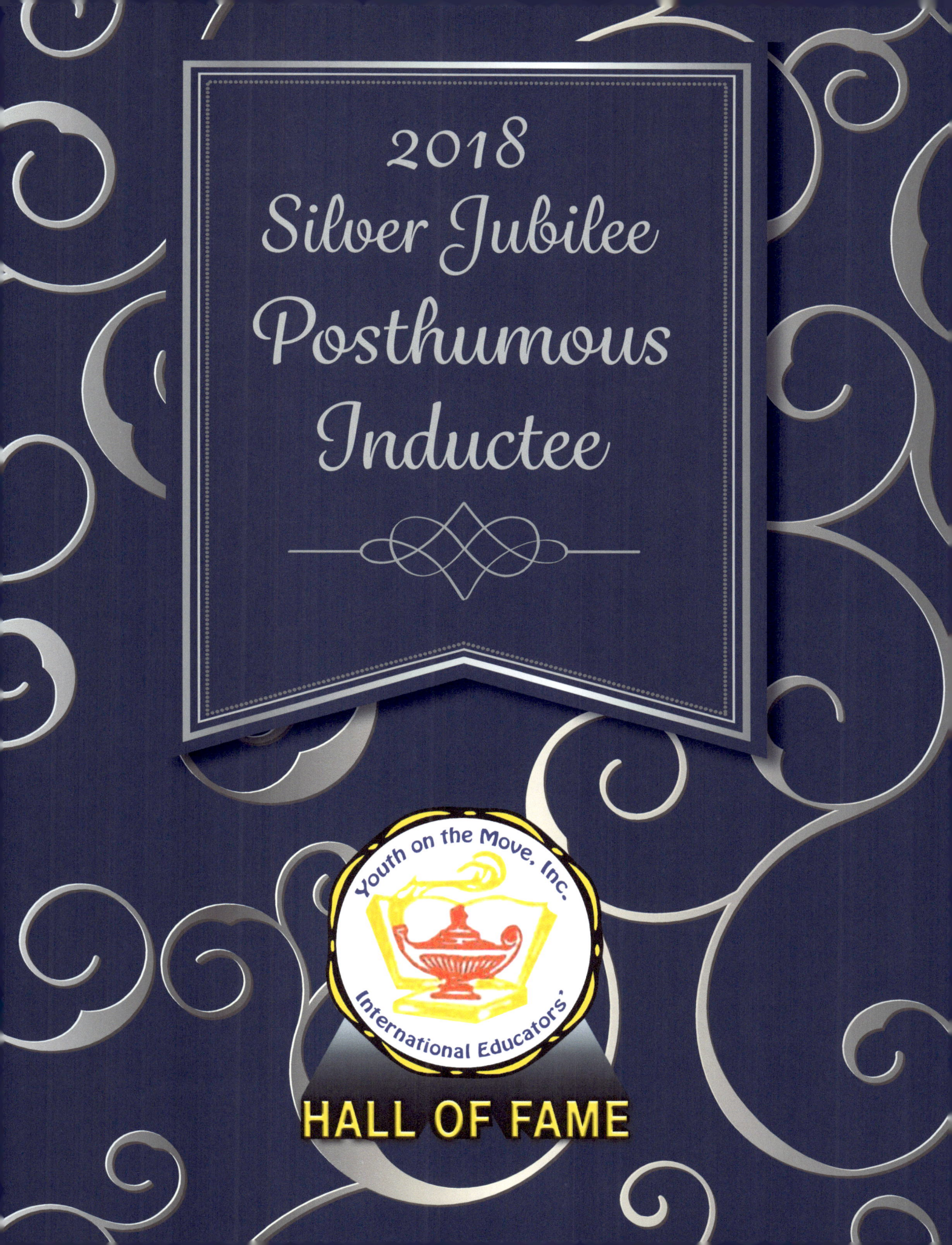

Julius Rosenwald

Born: Springfield, Illinois, August 12, 1862

Julius Rosenwald was born on August 12, 1862 in Springfield, Illinois to Jewish immigrant parents from Germany. He received his early education in Springfield, Illinois, not far from the Abraham Lincoln residence, during the Lincoln's Presidency of the United States.

By the time he was 16 years old, he entered the clothier business to learn the clothing trade and eventually he became a multimillionaire from this merchant trade and one of the founders of Sears, Roebuck, and Company – then the largest department store in the US.

Rosenwald was a friend and admirer of Booker T. Washington (founder of Tuskegee University and an Inductee in the International Educators' Hall of Fame). He was also a member of the Tuskegee Institute Board of Trustees. In 1911, after reading Washington's autobiography, Up From Slavery, Rosenwald convinced other wealthy white philanthropists to join him in setting aside a portion of the funds they donated to Tuskegee to be used to build black schools in rural Alabama.

Rosenwald felt that education was the key to African American progress. Thus, he was determined to support black education, not only in Alabama but throughout the South. And Black communities raised millions of dollars to contribute to the cause. Rosenwald established The Rosenwald Fund, in 1917 and through it, built over 5,300 schools, homes, and shops for a period of 25 years.

On July 30, 1948, the Julius Rosenwald Fund dissolved after twenty-five years of existence. Some Rosenwald Fund schools still stand across the South today and remain in use as community centers and registered historic sites.

The Tuskegee Institute – Rosenwald was asked to serve on the Board of Directors of the Tuskegee Institute in 1912. He endowed the Institute to free up Booker T. Washington from fundraising to devote more time managing the Institute.

An example of a Rosenwald school. By 1928 one in every five rural schools in the South was a Rosenwald school.

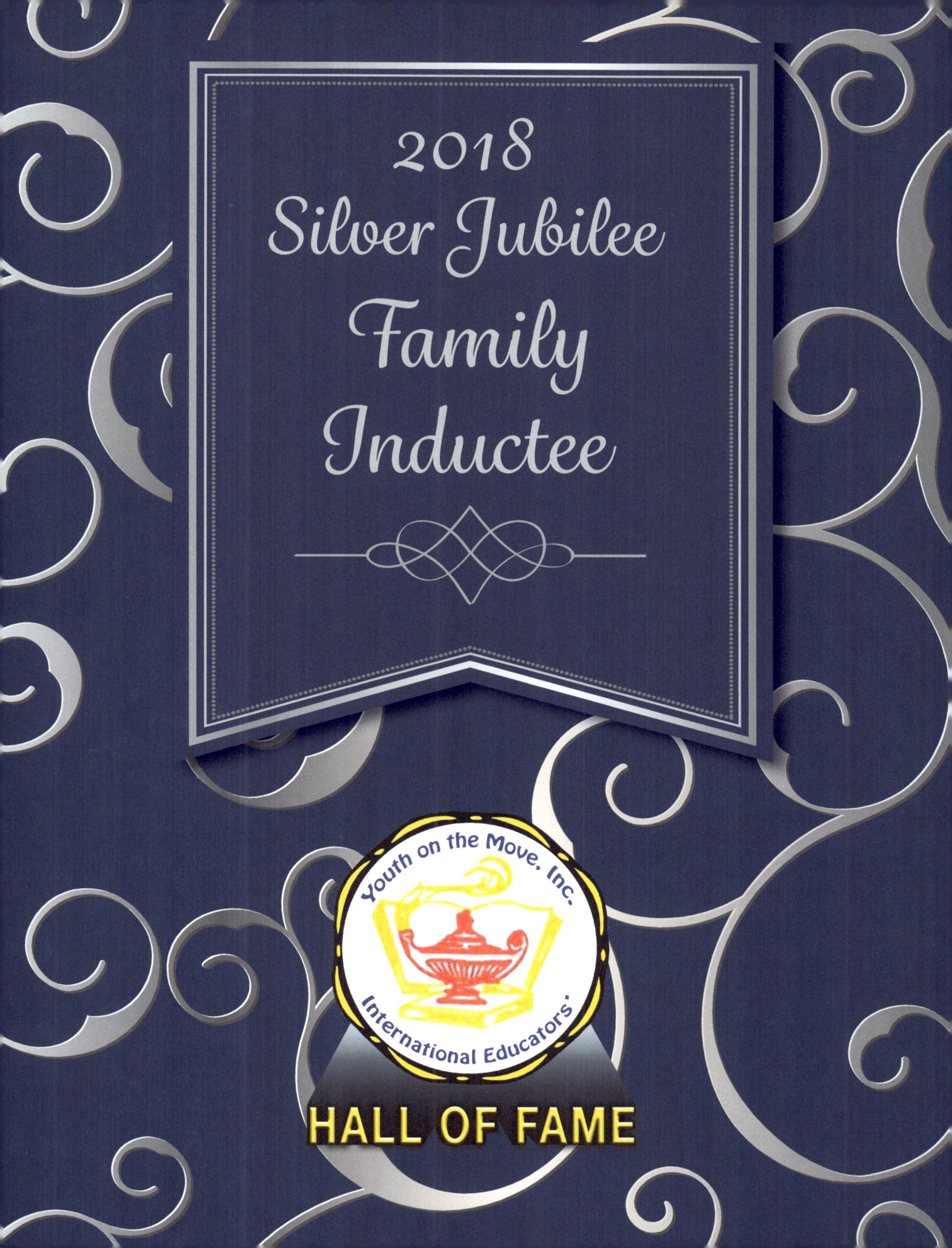

The Rick Gonzales Sr. Family

Standing: Garry, LaVerne, Rick Jr. and Jerry
Seated: Rick Gonzales Sr. and Angela Gonzales

Rick Gonzales Sr. served in WW II in Okinawa in the Pacific campaign. Upon his discharge, he enrolled in Barber School in San Francisco where he met his wife, Angela Duran. Together they had four sons, LaVerne, Garry, Rick Jr. and Jerry. In 1953, he opened Rick's Top Hat barbershop for business in Woodland.

Before this, Latinos had to travel to Sacramento because no one in Woodland would cuttheir hair. After their children grew up, Rick Sr. and Angela attended cosmetology classes to earn their licenses. They opened the Velvet Touch Beauty Salon. Soon their barber shop and beauty salon were a central hub of information on political and social issues. Small children hanging around these businesses were asking questions and finding inspiration to go out and change the world. Rick Sr. called these critical moments with people "teaching moments."

And so it was as generations of people, who thought they were going in for a haircut, came out with a new lease on life. Giving a voice to the "voiceless" and restoring hope to the disenfranchised of all races was Rick Sr.'s destiny. He had a natural talent for analyzing problems in helping others. A lifelong friend in the 70s, David Armendariz, gave Rick Sr. the nickname "The Godfather" because he was involved in many activities and truly embraced people as his own family. In fact, he would often introduce people as relatives when there was no blood relation, but to Rick Sr. this did not matter. He loved them and he claimed them.

Rick Gonzales Sr. and his entire family made many sacrifices of discretionary family time and income along the way. Hundreds of deserving students were guided toward the path of financial aid and professional success. Hundreds more received letters of recommendation to help them get good jobs. When asked to give five words to describe his father, Rick Jr. replied, "Dedication, Leadership, Equality for All, Compassionate, Negotiator."

Rick's wife, Angela, was at his side through his final days, comforted by the outpouring of untold stories and gratitude from hundreds who came forward to tell how her husband made a difference for them. He was one of the co-founders of the Mexican American Concilio of Yolo County, back in 1970 in Woodland. He became the Executive Director until his death in 2004. He had six full-time and other part-time employees who advocated for Latinos in finding jobs, education, translations, immigration, income taxes, housing, etc.

Rick Gonzales Jr.

Upon graduation from high school, Rick Jr. joined the US Army traveling to Germany and then Vietnam. Upon his discharge, he enrolled in Sacramento City College and then transferred to CSU, Sacramento where he received a BA and a secondary teaching credential in 1972. He started teaching at Sacramento High School in Special Education and was named the Boys Varsity Soccer Coach where he coached for eighteen years. In 1974, the Varsity Soccer Team was ranked number one in the state and invited to the California State Soccer Championships in La Jolla, CA.

He sent about fifty students to CSU, Sacramento for playing soccer at Sac High. His legacy at Sac High was that for fifteen years, every senior in his Special Education classes passed the regular High School Proficiency Test in English and Math. His students were eligible to take an alternative test, but Rick Gonzales Jr. wanted his students to pass the same test that everyone else had to pass. He raised the standards and every student reached those standards.

After 23 years at Sac High, he earned his Administrative Credential and became a VP at Luther Burbank HS for two years. He finished his 36 year teaching career by being a PE teacher in several elementary schools for eleven years, retiring in 2008.

In 1995, Rick Jr. joined the Concilio being appointed to the Board of Directors where he was later voted VP and then President in 2000. His father mentored him until his death in 2004. Rick Jr. started the scholarship program in 1998 with two scholarships. He planned the Annual Concilio Recognition Dinner & Scholarship Fundraiser in 1998 and did it for twenty years. He added more scholarships as the years went by. He started with four sponsors and increased it to 120. The Concililo serves twelve high schools and continuation high schools as well as Woodland Community College and UC Davis, all in Yolo County.

Currently, the Concilio awards sixty scholarships each year so that promising students, mainly Latino, can attend college. Each school receives multiple scholarships. Including the seniors who will graduate in 2018, the Concilio will have awarded its 1000th scholarship for the past twenty years. The criteria to earn a Concilio scholarship are a high GPA, school or community service and financial need. Concilio has raised over $400,000 to pay for these 1000 scholarships. Rick Jr. is retiring in 2018 from the Concilio. A transition process will take place. Rick Jr. is glad that the scholarship program will continue but under new leadership.

Rick Gonzales Sr. valued education all his life. Although he only got to fifth grade in school, he and his wife raised four sons, three of whom earned Masters Degrees. Two of them became teachers, one became a police chief and the other is a successful business owner. LaVerne and Rick Jr. were the teachers. Jerry was the police chief and Garry, the owner of a Singer Sewing Machine Repair Shop in Chicago. Each son raised their own families. Because of Rick Sr.' community activism, Yolo County named the Department of Social Services the Rick Gonzales Building.

The City of Woodland also named the newest park, the Rick Gonzales Sr. Park in 2018, fourteen years after he passed away. Rick Gonzales Sr. is also the only individual to win the Liberty Bell Award twice given by the Yolo County Bar Association. This award is given to a non-lawyer who has helped the youth of Yolo County.

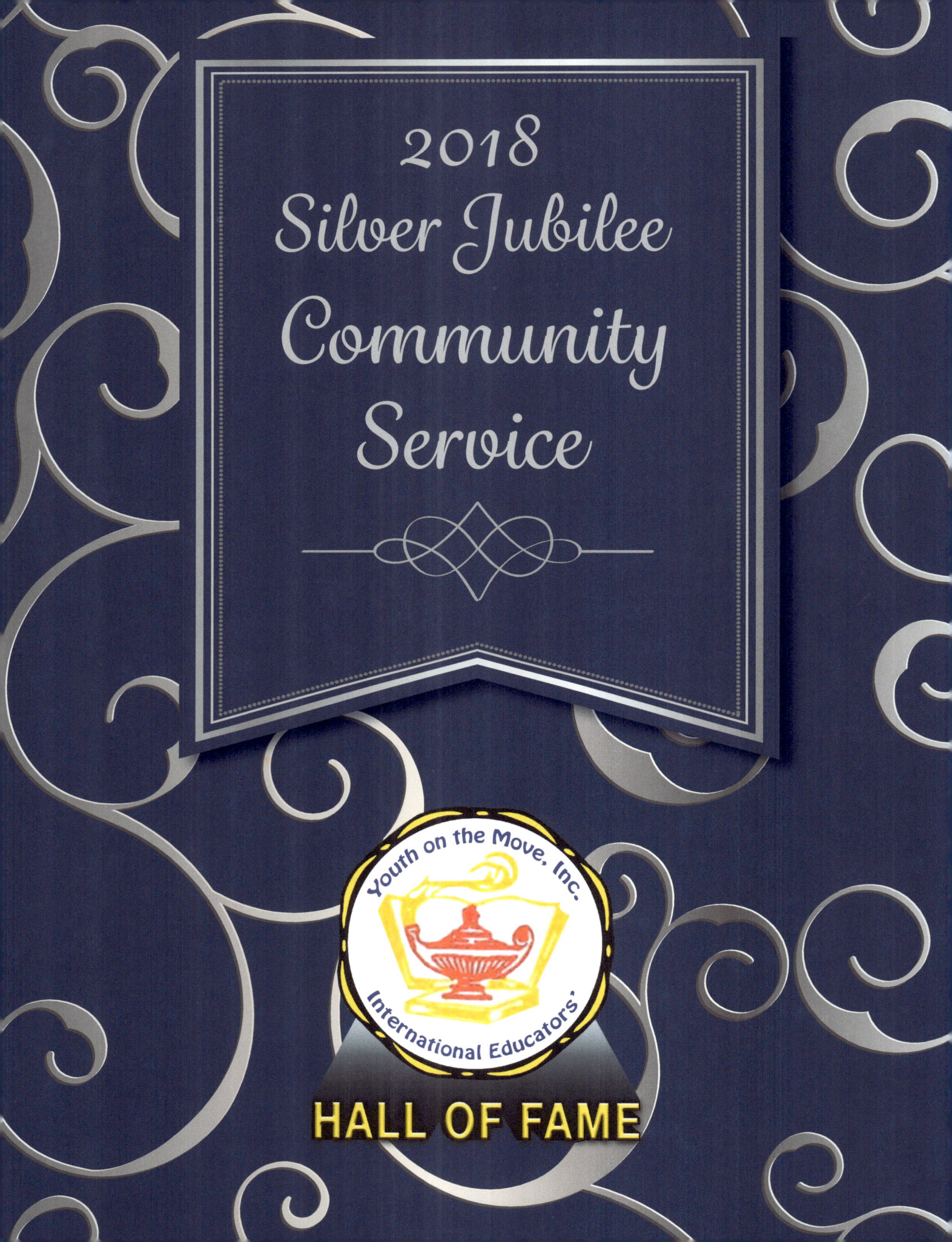

**The Youth-on-the-Move, Inc., Board of Directors recognizes the following community members who demonstrate through
their activities, services, and behavior interests in education, educators, families, and students.**

They are often "movers-and-shakers," "founders," and positive role models.

Mr. Mikhail Kishchenko

Youth Pastor, Slavic Missionary Church

Mr. Mikhail is the Youth Pastor of the Slavic Missionary Church in Sacramento, California.

He spent the first 15 years of his life in the Ukraine, and while still young, his mother encouraged him to learn and gather experiences and knowledge to be able to help his generation.

He came to the United States in his early life. When he was a teenager, many of his close friends "turned to the world," he says, "and, I turned to the Lord and became spiritually involved with the church and other positive actions which led to my being respected and admired by my elders and Pastors."

Today, he has been appointed the Youth Overseer/leader for the state of California to unite Slavic and non-Slavic youth in efforts towards harmony and a positive actions in the community. He is currently organizing and leading a youth conference for the Slavic youth in all 50 states. And he preaches the main word on Sundays in his local and other churches.

His advice to youth: "Every young and old person needs to get to know the Holy Spirit as a best and personal friends . . .and trust is the Holy Spirit to guide you to the right relationships, and you will fulfill the will of God with His guidance and grace.

His favorite quote: ". . . but the people who know their God shall be strong, and carry out exploits." Daniel 11:32.

Mr. Mikhail Kishchenko is married with three children. "My wife is my biggest and greatest supporter in my calling and my ministries. She is amazing and strong," he says.

Mr. & Mrs. Samuel Lesley Oliver

Mr. Samuel Lesley and Dorothy Oliver are the owners of the California Motor Escort & Patrol Co. based in Oakland and Sacramento, California. Mr. Oliver started the motor cycle and security business in 1974 in Oakland, CA. and a few years later, established an office in South Sacramento.

Mrs. Dorothy Oliver was owner and operator of Dorothy's Care Home from 1987 to 2000 in Sacramento. Her care home served numerous children with disabilities; she helped to educate, mentor, and train, not only the students with disabilities, but also, Youth-on-the-Move, Inc. (YOMI) youths. In this capacity, YOMI youth became role models, mentors, and peer tutors themselves.

These two businesses contributed greatly to the functions and outreach of Youth-on-the-Move, Inc. They sponsored T-shirts, programs, activities – and the Motor and Escort company often escorted (at no cost) parades and activities of YOMI's British Double Decker Bus which served as a community service vehicle, consulting with parents and families and serving the youths. Mr. & Mrs. Oliver had children, grandchildren, nieces and nephews who were and are still active members of YOMI – four generations of a family belonging to YOMI.

Today, those youths who were 5-12 years old then, are today 35-45 years old – bringing up their own children, many of whom have won 4-year full scholarships to institutions like the Universities of California Davis, Irvine and Berkeley, and others. "We learned how to help them, by belonging to YOMI," says Mrs. Dorothy Oliver and her sister, Denesia Bobo.

Bonnie Jean Pannell
Sacramento City Council (Posthumous)

Bonnie Jean Pannell was an exemplary City Council Woman who served on the Sacramento City Council from 1998 to 2014 (16 years). She filled the vacancy of the Council seat left by her husband –Councilman Samuel C. Pannell who had passed in December, 1997. Samuel was also an outstanding politician and educator, and was honored by the International Educators' Hall of Fame in 1997, after his death.

With such devoted public servants representing District 8 in Sacramento, it is no wonder that the Board of Directors of the International Educators' Hall of Fame, found it fitting and proper to honor Bonnie C. Pannell during their 25 year anniversary (Silver Jubilee) event.

Thank you, Bonnie C. Pannell for being the stalwart role model and servant of the people that you were. When we travel in your District (District 8) along Meadowview Road, we cannot help but see the development encouraged by you and the beauty and service that such development creates (the Regional Transit's Light Rail South Line Phase I and II, the Cosumnes River Boulevard through to Interstate Highway-5 and the shops, the signs "Delta Shores," etc.)

Thank you. May your soul rest in Peace with your husband, Samuel C. Pannel and daughter, Bridgitti A. Pannell – where we all hope to go one day. You are a role model for many.

Derrell and Tina Roberts
Roberts Family Development Center (RFDC)

In 1987, Derrell was a community advocate who led teams of youths in sports and other activities in the Oak Park area of Sacramento. During his time there, he was one of the volunteers and mentors at Youth-on-the-Move, Inc. "I will never forget him," says Dr. Patricia Adelekan. "During the summer when 'Tokunbo Adelekan, my son, came home from Morehouse College, Derrell would have a summer job for him – to keep him busy, out of trouble and with a few dollars in his pocket. What a blessing, I shall never forget."

It is wonderful to see Derrell and his wife, Tina, running the Roberts Family Development Center. They began the Center in 2001 as a way to strengthen families and to guide individual family members to success by concentrating on each person's needs

Three of their famous programs are (1) The Freedom School: a summer literacy program designed by National Children Defense Fund to encourage young scholars to read.

(2) Black Child Legacy Campaign: a 3-year initiative to reduce the high incidents of death of African American infants/youth. RFDC works with various community partners to incorporate several community strategies for success.

(3) Parent Empowerment: a program involving educational experts to provide parents with tools to become effective advocates for their children.

A favorite quote: "Education is the most powerful weapon which you can use to change the world." *Nelson Mandela.*

Their advice to young people: "You can be anything you want, if you work hard at it."

Mr. Richard Nelson
Founder, HAWK youth group

The resolution by the City of Sacramento dated September 26, 2016, highlights a number of my achievements. In addition, there is the following: I was born in Houston, Texas, December 24,1949, raised in Berkeley, California, graduated from Chico State in 1972 with a Bachelor's degree in sociology. I am the father of 3 living sons and one daughter, all of whom graduated from college. Growing up, my life was heavily influenced by my father Richard L. Nelson and his sister, my aunt, Imogene Cork. I would encourage young people to think big, work hard, and maintain a strong moral compass. As a parent, we should always take care of our children both emotionally and financially.

Mr. Rick Warren

Rick Warren Media

Rick Warren has been one of the chief mentors and motivators of Dr. Patricia Ann Adelekan. In the early 1990's, he taught her how to plan, develop and layout and design a Youth-on-the-Move newspaper entitled Youth-on-the-News. He is a community role model who demonstrates how communities can work together.

Rick is creative and imaginative. He is the founder of many successful entities: the Black Music Association; the Black Expo in three cities; the Black Sports Hall of Fame; the Minorities N Real Estate Expo; the Gospel RIVERFEST; and the Oak Park Spring Festival. For over 25 years, he was a former editor of the Sacramento Observer Newspaper. Currently, he is the publisher and President of the Today's Times Newspaper which focuses on issues affecting the African American Community. Recently, he celebrated the 30th Anniversary of the Sacramento Black History Month Black Expo. He is a compassionate, gifted and "giving" community educator.

Alpha Bruton Family

Alpha M. Bruton is the mother. They joined YOMI in 1985 (as a family) They are foundation members.

TaShant D. Raney Esq, May 27, 1977 (41) (he was 8 when he joined).Resides in Fresno CA, Graduated from Sacramento High School, 1995 studied Sociology at CSU Sacramento, Dominguez Hills

Herbert E. Raney, August 8, 1978 (40) (he was 7 when he joined). Graduated from Redondo Beach High School, United States Air Force, NCO Master Sergant. Stationed Mascoutah Illinois at Scott's Airforce Base. Twenty year career 2007-2018.

Jazmin Bruton Davis, March 5, 1986 (32) (she joined at age 1)

Graduated Crete Monee High, 2004. Florida Memorial 2006, Graduated

Steven G. Lawrence and Family

Steven Lawrence and his children,
10 years old then – 40 today, singer, writer.

Cory Moore, 16 then – 44 now
(Khiry Malik Moore)

Some Famous Hall of Famers

Wilson Riles '92
First Black Superintendent of Schools, CA

Jaime Escalante '93
Teacher; Main character in movie "Stand and Deliver"

Jack Forbes, Ph.D. '96
UC Davis, American Artist

David Risling, M.A. '94
Founder, D.Q. University

Benjamin S. Bloom, Ph.D. '98
Founder, Bloom's Taxonomy; Head Start;
Master Learning Theory

Cornel West, Ph.D. '98
Princeton/ Harvard; Professor, Philosopher,
Author, Race Matters

Carolyn Stokes, M.A. '99
Founder, Bay Area YOMI Hall of Fame

Paulo Freire, Ph.D. '13
Pedagogy of the Oppressed (1970)

Al Jenkins, Esq., '96
Founder, "Pass the CA Bar the First Time"

Lucia Birnbaum, Ph.D. '96
Researcher/Professor, Black Madonna

Jose Montoya, '96
Artist, poet, educator

Magda Moussa – Egypt '96
Founder, Misr Language School,
Director, Special Olympics, Egypt

Howard Thurman, '96
Founder, author, philosopher, theologian, educator

Frank Withrow, '95
Teacher Rapper, Poet

Dr. Lottie C. Blake, '13
Medical Missionary, Teacher

Louis Johnson, Jr., '92
Teacher, Vocalist

John & Kathryn Favors Ph.Ds., '93
Founders – Thematic Integrated
Education (Curriculum) TIE

Anyim Palmer, Ph.D. '94
Founder, Marcus Garvey School, LA

Dr. B. Roberto Cruz '95
Founder, National Hispanic University, San Jose, CA

Sarah H. Hutchison, '95
Pioneer, American Indians at the Smithsonian

Mary Tsuruko Tsukamoto, '95
Teacher, Pioneer, Japanese Reparations and
Presence at the Smithsonian

Ralph C. Smedley, '13
Founder, Toastmasters International

Estaban Villa, '96
Professor Emeritus, CSUS,
Founder, Royal Chicano Airforce,
Artist, Writer, Muarlist

Asa Hilliard, '98
Historian, Egyptologist, Educational Administer

Dr. William H. Lee '98
Founder, Sacramento Observer Newspapers

Honorable Samuel Pannell, '98
Founder, City Council

Dr. Robert H. Schuller, '01
Founder, Crystal Cathedral,
Possibility Thinking Minister

Confucius, '01
Philosopher, Teacher - China

Carl Gorman, '01
Code Talkers (WWII) – Artist

Dr. Lewis Jackson '13
Director of Training that prepared Tuskegee Airman

Professor Isao Fujimoto, Ph.D., 16
Developed the UC Davis's Course on Human Development,
International Scholar

Justice Cruz Reynoso, 16
Frist, Chicano to be appointed to the California Court of
Appeals and to the Supreme Court

Amin David, '16
Founder, Los Amigos, Anaheim

Mr. L Ron Hubbard, '15
Founder, Applied Scholastics

Ltd. Colonel Alexander Jefferson, '15
A Tuskegee Airman

Dr. Essie French-Preston, '16
Distinguished Faculty, El Camino College, Compton Center,
Educator of the Year, Phi Delta Kappa.

Booker T. Washington, '99
American Educator, Founder of Tuskegee Institute
Friend to Julius Rosenwald (Rosenwald Schools)

Dr. Kogee Thomas '14
Educator, Founder of Lobo Lodge
Native American Museum

W.E.B. Du Bois, '15
First African American to earn a Ph.D. Degree
From Harvard University at age 26

Barbara L. and Nathan K. Banda '16
Teacher, Acjachemen Nation

Carl C. Mack, Jr., Ph.D, '16
Associate Professor Alliant International University

Amin David, 16
Community Educator, Los Amigos OC

Inductees 2018

Individual

Dr. Florin John Ciuriuc
Holly S. Cooper
Edenausegboye Beulah Pearl Davis, MPA
Dr. Kevin Russell Gibbs
Mr. Raymond Gutierrez, Jr.
Dr. Desmond Jolly
Jeraldine "Jerri" Lange
Aladrian Mack, M.A.
Mrs. Diane Chandler-Marshall, M.A.
Doris I. Mangrum
Mrs. Jacque Sherrill Tahuka-Nunez, B.A., B.S.
Amagda Pérez, Esq.
Linda D. Rose, Ed.D.
Dr. Elmer L. Towns, Dean. MIN.
Harold Dean Trulear, Ph.D.
Holly Viola Van Valkenburgh

International

Dr. Kaanchanapalli Govardhan Raju, M.A., MPhil, Ph.D.
Dr. Juan Carlos Ortiz

Posthumous

Julius Rosenwald

Family

The Rick Gonzales, Sr. Family

Community Service Awards

Mr. Mikhail Kishchenko; Youth Pastor, Slavic Missionary Church
Mr. Eric Murrell, Murrell's Fashion
Mr. Richard Nelson; Co-Founder, HAWK youth group
Mr. & Mrs. Oliver, California Motor & Escort Company
Bonnie Jean Pannell; Sacramento City Council (Posthumous)
Mr. & Mrs. Darrell Roberts; Roberts Family Development Center
Mr. Rick Warren, RW Media

Program

Saturday, July 7, 2018 10:00 AM – 4:00 PM

EmCees:

Jasmine M. Johnson, Dr. Patricia Adelekan, Dr. Connie Cooper, Cynthia Moreno

10:00 a.m.	Doors Open, Registration Braclets: Florence • Hall of Famers IEHOF Special Sign-in: Johnny Dale Ciuriuc Corsages: Yelena Gavrilyuk Table/Seating USHERS – Mikhail Kishchenko Inside Exhibit Room – Silent Auction, Meet the Inductees, View Exhibits, Continental Breakfast
11:30 a.m.	Program Starts – EmCees, Pledge of Allegiance, Joshua F. Ciuriuc, USA, Ukraine, Romania, Mexico, India, Argentina, The Acjachemen Nation, Jamaica Stand still while National Anthem plays
Noon	Invocations (2min each): Host Ivan Gavrilyuk from Slavic Missionary Church; Rev. Dr. Lawrence Wilkes, Founder Trinity Christian Schools; Rev. Sadler, Senior Pastor, Shiloh Baptist Church; Jacque Nunez, Acjachemen Nation; Pastors Martin & Zoila Barraza, Los Angeles.
12:15 p.m.	Recognition of the VIPS and Sponsors: Rick Warren, RW Media
12:20 p.m	Welcome – Bishop Adam Bondaruk, Senior Pastor Slavic Missionary Church
12:25 p.m.	History and Purpose of the Hall of Fame: Patricia Adelekan, Ph.D., Founder
12:30 p.m.	Inductees, Powerpoint, 2 minutes each, Mahendar Adluri & Ivan Gavrilyuk Line up of VIP Greeters: Al Wilson, Board of Directors, IEHOF; Bishop Adam Bondaruk, Senior Pastor, Slavic Missionary Church, Ivan, Dr. Patricia Adelekan, Founder, Youth-on-the-Move, Inc. Pledge of all new Hall of Famers, Alumni Hall of Famers gather – Pass on the Torch, Bring into Fold
1:30 p.m.	Youth Awards – YOMI Youth – Mr. Sadler
1:35 p.m.	Performers: Slavic Choral
1:15 p.m.	Remarks by a 2018 Hall of Famer – Rick Warren, RW Media and Jasmine M. Johnson – RYTMO
1:45 p.m.	Closing Remarks, Dr. Patricia Adelekan, Founder
1:50 p.m.	Group Photographs; Ivan, Bishop, All 2018 Hall of Famers Present, Board of Directors and 2018 Committee members, All Youth, Others until 2:00 p.m. Adjournment

2:00 pm. – 4:00 p.m.

You are cordially invited to lunch in Room #2 and to network with one another across the way; take tours of this facility. Thank you for coming and Congratulations!

33 Years
Youth-On-the-Move
1985 – 2018

HALL OF FAME

Goals and purposes of Yomi Tutorial Program

Youth-on-the-Move, Inc. (YOMI - 1987)

1. To offer additional help to school-age youth in the areas of mathematics, reading, spelling, vocational skills, the arts, science, self esteem building, cultural histories, and computers.
2. To help improve multi-cultural relations among youth, their families, the community and the schools.
3. To serve as a liaison between the family and the school in order to improve the home/school relationships and student performance in the academic and social world. We work with parents/guardians, students, community, the church, business, law enforcement agencies, role models and schools to reach this goal.
4. To train and encourage youth to be ambassadors of the YOMI spirit and mission wherever they go.
5. To train youth to be PEER TUTORS and ROLE MODELS reaching back and out to positively help other youth in the academic areas.
6. To assist schools in carrying out their goals and plans for effectiveness.

Our Major Purpose is to Work with Students Already in School (grades 1-16) BUT OTHERS ARE WELCOME

TALENT IN THE ARTS

The purposes of this component are to:

- To help develop the artistic abilities and creativity in YOMI youth
- To identify youth who have artistic talents
- To promote, expose and refer artistically talented YOMI youth (budding performing and/or visual artist/video producers) to the public and/or to public and private agencies
- To produce talented YOMI youth (whenever possible)
- To expose YOMI youth to the arts of various cultures
- To promote the use of the arts for learning and problem solving
- To promote and produce at least two major artistic performances each year
- To encourage interaction among a wide variety of youths, adults, community organizations, universities, businesses and others who have been interested in the arts (performing/visual video).

Some Participants Through the Years

- Aca Sato
- Adebayo Adelekan
- Adebola Adelekan
- Adebola Adelekan, Esq
- Adedotun Adelekan
- Adedoyin Adelekan
- Adenike Adelekan
- Adenike Adelekan
- Adeola Adelekan
- Adrianna Cerda
- Al Wilson
- Alan Gold
- Alan J Pimentel
- Albert Hicks
- Alejandra Cabrera
- Allen Wickham
- Allison C Wilcut
- Alpha Bruton
- Alpha Bruton
- Alpha Diallo
- Alyssa Rodriguez
- Amani Moore
- Amezcua
- Amogh Adluri
- Andrea Hernandez
- Andrea Vega
- Andrew Hernandez
- Andy Au
- Angela Ayala
- Anita M Hernandez
- April Pineda
- Attorney Joseph Cooper
- Avery Maier
- Ayleen Perez
- Barbara Reynolds
- Baron Reed
- Beckie
- Ben Pham
- Benjamin Frias
- Bennie Ellis
- Bertha Udell
- Beth Clayson
- Bill Boyer
- Blanka Robles
- Bonnie Pannell
- Brianna Baleanu
- Brisa Cruz-Miranda-Rifle
- Bros-Alfonso
- Bryan Placido
- Bryan Placido-Flag
- Buddy Solomon
- Callista S Pattillo
- Camico McKnight
- Camisha Abels
- Carissa Saucedo
- Carlos Farias
- Carlos Saucedo
- Carrie Moore
- Celine Flores
- Chloe Chafin
- Christian Bnassell
- Chuckie Gilliam
- Cindy Guzman
- Cinthia Aguilar
- Cleste Esquivias
- Cody Chavira
- Cole Wilkes
- Cris Rosales
- Cynthia Reynoso
- Daniel Ayala
- Danielle Cuayahuitl
- Dante Garcia
- Dave Machewiski
- David Thomas Montoya
- Derrell Roberts
- Derrick Brooks
- Diamond Payton
- Diedra Butler
- Dorothy Oliver
- Dr. Bill Lee
- DuJuan Moore
- Dulce Aguillar
- Dustin Guinee
- Dylan Gardner
- Eduardo Martinez Flore
- Edvin Perez
- Edward Belmontez
- Elkins Servin-Flag
- Emily Aguillar
- Emily D Buck
- Emily Frisan
- Emily Hinojoza
- Emmanuel Soria
- Eric Murrell
- Erina McCoy
- Faith Medina
- Francisco Alfaro
- Frank Diaz Jimenz
- Frank Withrow
- Gabriel F Alarid
- Gboyega Adelekan
- Gene McElhannon
- Genevy Narvaez
- Ghazal Barikzai
- Gibran Cerezo
- Gillian Urban
- Gisela Flores-Singer
- Giselle Aguilar
- Glenda Willis
- Gwen Barrios
- Harvey Branner
- Hayden Dunham
- Hilario Aranda
- Hyacinth Thomson
- Isabel Trujillo
- Isabel V Hernandez
- Isabella Rojas
- Isai Navarro
- Itzel Vera
- Iva Chavez
- Jaclyn K Scoggins
- Jade Liu Elissa
- Monterroso
- Jade Victor Arbilon S
- Jakob Dcameron
- Jamal
- James Burnell
- Janine Johnson
- Jannah Zahir
- Jaqueline Vera
- Jason Banks
- Jazmine Reyes
- Jenny Truong
- Jeremy Pamplona
- Jessica Cervantes
- Jessica Garcia
- Jessica Miller Russell
- Jessioca Morales
- Jesus Eugenio
- Joe R Ortiz
- Johanna Perez
- John Strother
- John Strother
- Jonathan Martinez
- Jonathan Ponce
- Jose Cadenas
- Jose Castaneda
- Jose Cuevas
- Joseph Bautista
- Joseph M Bustamante
- Joseph Montoya
- Joseph Ruhl-Flag
- Joshua D Solis
- Julia Powers
- Julian Rodriguez
- Kaitlyn N Tenerio
- Karen Massey
- Kayal Meek
- Kayumi Loch
- Kelly Avalos
- Kendra J Egland
- Kevin Gomez
- Khalod Teamer
- Khiry Core Moore
- Kimberly G Macias
- Lannah M Martin
- Larry Lee
- Larry Lee
- Leland Johnson
- Lerryn McCullough
- Lesley Velasco
- Lesley Oliver
- Leslie Ramirez
- Leslie Vargas
- Lesly Lezama
- Lexi Thi
- Lexie F Ebel
- Linda C Salgado
- Linda Jaeckels
- Lizeth Gelacio
- Lizette Tapia
- Lois McDaniel
- Loren Reed
- Lucille J Martinez
- Luis Carapia
- Mae Watson
- Mahender Adluri
- Mahita Adluri
- Makenah Harris
- Malea Schnell
- Mandalyn Valasquez
- Maria Avila
- Maria Cuellar
- Maria Torres
- Maricruz Quezeda
- Marissa Golden
- Marissa Torres
- Mark B. Thomas
- Mark V Halsig
- Mary Moore
- Mary Nguye
- Megan A Koontz
- Melissa Hasbun
- Mertie Shelby
- Mia De Anda
- Mia Fuentes
- Mia Villalvazo
- Michael Magana
- Michael Pelton
- Miguel Perez
- Miguel Perez
- Mike del la Pena
- Milad Ataei
- Miles A Chapman
- Monica Vasquez
- Monroe Mitchell
- Morgan B Dodero
- Myriam Grande
- Nancy Nunez
- Natalia M Gradillas
- Nathaniel Thomas
- Neil Hollander
- Nicco May
- Nicholas Mulder
- Nicole Naveja
- Nicole Reyes
- Nohelia Chavez
- Oliver Solares
- Olvia And Sophia
- Patricia Adelekan Dr.
- Patricia Solomon
- Phuong Tran
- Rachel Wilson
- Reem Saad
- Releyna Wickham
- Remi Adelekan
- Reylenya Wickham
- Rhonda Fletcher
- Ricardo Bautista
- Richard Nelson
- Rick Warren
- Rnad Ridha
- Roberto Ramirez-Flag
- Rodrigo Camacho
- Rodriguez
- Rudy Acevedo
- Sade Adelekan
- Sade Adelekan
- Samantha Calderon
- Samantha Stapish-Higa
- Samuel Pannell
- Santana Del Castillo
- Sara Von Davenport
- Savannah Erica
- Savannah Johnson
- Schwartz
- Sennie Viramontes
- Shaina Trujillo-Flag
- Shari Mailler
- Sheyla Mendoza
- Sholanda King
- Sholanda King
- Sophia Holguin
- Stephani Herrera-Hughes
- Stephanie A Chavez
- Stephanie Aguilar
- Stephanie Chavez
- Steven Lawrence
- Tokumbo Adelekan
- Tom Burrus
- Tracy Tran
- Tricia Miles
- Trisha Lim
- Valaria Flores
- Veronica Saurez
- Vickki Walker
- Victor Rivera-Rifle
- Von Roy
- Wonda Scott
- Yadira Hernandez
- Yulianna Matta
- Zackerie Noeman
- Zafiro Hernandez
- Zenobia Todd
- Zenobia Todd
- Zettia Barney

Mission Statement and Creed

Youth-On-The-Move, Inc. (YOMI) is a 501 (c)(3) non-for-profit multi-cultural youth education organization aimed to empower youth to succeed in school, the work world, and life in general - with the help of positive community role models.

Creed

1. I believe that I am special. I am the most important person I know.

2. I believe in a drug-free body that leads to a free mind.

3. I believe I should respect my fellowman, and be a good citizen.

4. I believe in strength and unity.

5. I believe I should trust in God.

6. I believe in setting goals and believing in myself.

7. I believe I should have dreams of positive mental attitude to be successful.

8. I believe in treating people the way I like to be treated.

9. This is my creed I want to achieve so help me God.

This creed was developed by about 20 Youth-On-The-Move, Inc., (YOMI) youth members in 1987 with the assistance of a senior mentor (age 71 at the time), Dr. Clarice Isaac (Hall of Famer '94). Each student had a turn in saying what he/she believed in - after spending about one hour combining and revising their beliefs, they came up with this creed.

YOMI was incorporated in February of 1986 to promote artistic talent, job training and educational tutoring ("the three T's") for youth in grades K through 12. The organization's tutorial program had grown into a first-class preparatory academy serving youth in grades 7 through 12.

Yomi Prep. Academy students

Hall of Famers: Ida Sunson '94, Dr. Kathryn Favors '93, Carolyn Stokes '93

The Mahender Adluri Family

A photo of Denesia Bobo and her Grandson, Ferrick Moore, and Dr. Patricia Adelekan, YOMI founder and CEO. Ferrick's mom, also Patricia, joined YOMI when she was 7 years old; now (2018) she is 40 and Ferrick (her son) is a sophomore at UC Irvine in Orange County, California on a 4 year-full scholarship.

Amogh Adluri

Skills and Talent: knows all the capitals of the world, loves solving all kinds of rubiks cubes, was student of the month every year

Experience on Youth-on-the-Move: went with father to many Youth on the Move meetings

Best memory on Youth-on-the-Move: drawing flags of countries for Hall of Fame

Mahita Adluri

Skills and Talent: sketching, drawing, knows a lot about animals

Experience on Youth-on-the-Move: went with father to many youth on the move meetings

Best memory on Youth-on-the-Move: displayed her sketches for Youth-on-the-Move

Miguel Perez

Families in Yomi

This is a family (3 generations) that belong to YOMI since 1987 – our beginning. Today, those youths are in their 40's with their own children (all University students with FULL SCHOLARSHIPS) and helping others. YOMI, specializes in academics and aide for children with disabilities. We are intergenerational and family oriented.

Mother: Denesia Bobo, age 63, valiant administrator at a care home for disabled children and active mother participant in Youth on the Move Inc(Yomi).

Denesia Bobo had three children (listed below) starting with her oldest to youngest who were also apart of Yomi in the year 1987

1. Gregory C. Gilliam, II (Chuckie). age 42, working two jobs one at a psychiatric hospital in Sacramento and another at a health clinic. Nine years old when he joined Yomi.

Chuckie's Children

Alyssa Gilliam, age 21, received four year scholarship to UC Davis now a registered nurse (RN)

Gregory C. Gilliam, III, age 19, currently attending the University of California, Berkeley with a four year full ride scholarship. Class of 2017. High school graduate of Sacramento Charter High School

Caleb I. Gilliam, age 12 in the 9th grade at Sacramento Charter High School

2. Patricia Solomon, age 40, self employed Tax Preparer at Public, Mail and More with a Masters in Business. Seven years old when she joined Yomi.

Patricia's Children

Ferrick Moore, age 19, currently attending the University of California, Irvine in pursuit of becoming a Radiologist as a Biological Science major. Received around $6,000 in scholarships. Class of 2017. High school graduate of Sacramento Charter High School, prior ASB Vice President of the high school.

Najeeb Peavy, age 10 in the fourth grade

3. William Solomon, III(Buddy), age 39, self employed personal fitness trainer. Six years old when he joined Yomi.

Buddy's Children

William Solomon, IV, age 12, in the 7th grade elected school president at Sutter Middle School
Ava, age 2, adorable darling

Grand Mother: Dorthy Oliver, age 75, owner and operator of Care Home fore Disabled Children

Father: Lester Oliver owner and operator of California Motor Escort and Patrol

Grandchildren of the Oliver's who were also in Yomi:
Nicki Oliver
Leslie Oliver

The Adelekan Family

Dr. Adetunji and Dr. Pat Adelekan, and children, Nigeria, 1983

Dr. Pat Adelekan, and children, Sacramento, CA, 1985

The Adelekan Family – Founding Family (Dr. Patricia Adelekan and children) 1985 in Sacramento, CA

Adebola Adelekan; age 17 then; now age 50 in 2018, A licensed lawyer in Los Angeles

Adetokunbo Adelekan: age 16 then; now age 49, Ph.D. in Theology and Ethics from Princeton, Head Pastor in Dayton, Ohio

Aderemi Adelekan: age 11 then; now age 44; IT Manager for Dish-AT&T

Adegboyega Adelekan: age 6 then; now age 39; Lawyer for Sabal Law Firm; Costa Mesa, CA; Owner, Crowning Partners Corp

Testimonial Letter to Youth-on-the-Move

June 17, 2013

I want to express my gratitude to Youth On The Move for guiding and supporting me when I was young. Your organization provided me with a venue to showcase my talents and kept me focused on positive things. Your energy and spirit motivated and nurtured me.

When I was 17, I moved to Los Angeles to pursue my dream of being a singer, and at the age of 19, I landed a starring role in the ABC television mini-series *The Jacksons: An American Dream*, where I played the role of Jermaine Jackson. Shortly after that, I was accepted to UCLA where I majored in Ethnomusicology. While at UCLA, I was hired to sing lead on "In The Still Of The Night" in Whoopie Goldberg's "Sister Act II".

I loved many things about being in the entertainment business, but I remember feeling empty after I completed filming *The Jacksons.* The more success I had, the more and alone I felt. I was asked to host a children's television talk show in Milwaukee around the time *The Jacksons* aired on television, and it really made a difference in my life. We filmed the show at an inner city school in Milwaukee, in front of a large group of students. I told my true story. I shared some of the painful circumstances of my childhood, and I was surprised to see the effect that this had on the children. Many of the children were going through what I had gone through growing up, and I was asked to speak to a select group of students in private. These were the students who had been most affected by my story. I was surprised to see many of them crying as they shared their stories with me. One of those students has remained in contact with me until this day.

I decided to try teaching, so I applied to a program called Teach For America where graduates from Ivy League schools were placed in inner city schools to help inner city children. I was placed in a school in the Bronx, NY, where I taught 5th grade. The attacks of 9-11 happened during my first week of teaching. I didn't think that I would make a good teacher because I'd hated school. But in fact, teaching turned out to be the perfect job for me. I get bored very easily, so I had to make my class fun and exciting for my own sanity. At the end of the school year, I had brought the lowest-performing 5th grade class in the school up to the level of the top performing-class on the state exams. My students wrote me letters telling me how I'd made a difference in their lives, and I still have those letters.

My story has not been without its trials and tribulations, but I believe that there are always solutions to whatever problems we face. A lot of us focus on money and some of us are willing to kill and die for it, but I have never been about money. I've always been about passion. I believe that if I follow my passion, the money will come.

Khalid Teemer

Khalid Teemer's Mother

My name is Bertha Rose Udell. I have a BA in Modern African Studies from the University of California, with a minor in Education. I earned a Masters in Education in the Department of Educational Leadership and Policy Development (ELDP), and an Interim Administrative Credential from California State University Sacramento. My Master's project was on The Relationship Between Vocabulary Knowledge and the Academic Achievement Gap. I mention these credits first because my focus came about after my introduction to and work with Youth-on-the-Move, Inc.

In 1988, I became involved with Youth-on-the-Move, Inc. and Dr. Patricia Adelekan because of the work they did with my son, Khalid Teemer.

Our time with the organization was filled with new opportunities and experiences for the whole family. This helped me see the value of working with our children in various settings, as a parent or volunteer. I wanted to bring my best to our youth, so I obtained a teaching credential from the Rex and Margaret Fortune Project Pipeline. Pipeline was created to increase diversity in the teaching population.

After teaching for 2 years in California, I was accepted into the International Foundation for Education and Self-Help (IFESH) as an Educator for Africa. IFESH was created by Dr. Leon Sullivan to place college graduates in various capacities in countries of Africa and the world to help build infrastructure and competency in local communities. I was selected IFESH Teacher of the Year in 2002. My two year assign was in Benin, West Africa.

I returned to the U.S. and began to work at Parkway Elementary School in the Sacramento City Unified School District (SCUSD). In 2008, I received a plaque in recognition of being part of the "Dream Team" that worked tirelessly to raise student state test scores from the low 400s to the high 700s!!

I retired from the SCUSD in 2012, but continue to be involved. I remain a community activist. Some of my commitments are: Board Member of the Black United Fund (BUF), and organization that provides classes and assistance to people in starting Non-Profit organizations.

"Thanks" to Dr. Adelekan for being a role model who helped me experience the rewards in working with children and families. I continue this service today, and I LOVE it! Congratulations to Youth on the Move for 33 years of consistent service, and I wish you many, many more.

Youth-on-the-Move – where are they today?

Oussama Deeb

Dr. Patricia has taught me French in 2000, in Cerritos College, CA. Dr. Pat loved all her students regardless of faith, culture, color, and race. She tried to make students feel welcomed and capable. I was a 20 years old, international student at Cerritos College coming from Beirut, Lebanon; Dr. Pat was a motherly figure to me. She provided support on different levels. At one hand, she ran a rich interesting French class.

Dr. Pat sacrificed some of her free time to help us, the students, meet the course objectives. On the other hand, Dr. pat turned the classroom into a multi-cultural gathering. It was Ramadan; I was allowed to bring in snacks and juice to break my fast. I felt comfortable enough to pray, she allowed me to go to the back of the room and pray during times, which was not the case in other courses.

I truly admire Dr. Pat for all she did that made me feel at ease at a hard time of my life. Today, after almost 15 years, I hold a BA in Education and MA in Leadership; I am currently a Vice Principal at a school in Dubai, UAE. This week we are conducting induction sessions for teachers, I always share how Dr. Pat celebrated cultures in her class and how amazing that reflected among her students.

Tamu Nolfo

is a developmental psychologist and thought leader who brings expertise and lived experience in communities facing inequities in her pursuit of social justice through institutional and systems change.

For over twenty years, she has been engaged in power building efforts that synergize resources, facilitate equity-oriented decision making, and turn advocacy into outcomes. By prioritizing planning, research and evaluation practices that maximize stakeholder engagement, coalition building and strategic partnerships,

Dr. Nolfo has confronted the social determinants of health at the community, state and national level. These efforts have been aided by her networks which include the Robert Wood Johnson Foundation and American Leadership Forum, of which she is a senior fellow.

Dr. Nolfo currently serves The Center at Sierra Health Foundation and the California Department of Public Health's Office of Health Equity, where she has been instrumental in developing and implementing the inaugural California Statewide Plan to Promote Health and Mental Health Equity.

Youth-on-the-Move – where are they today?

Ricardo Gonzales

Experience in Youth-On-The-Move, Inc.:

• Assisting the logistics for the International Educators Hall of Fame Inductee Ceremony

• Showing the inductees, their families, and friends to their seats

• Making the ceremony flow

Best memory was inducting all of the individuals into the International Educators Hall of Fame. Being able to hear their different stories was something special. Rewarding those who have done so much for our community was a reward in itself.

My Future Goal is to show people that no matter what kind of background you come from, you can always make a positive impact on the lives around us.

Rosalie Martinez

2nd Grade Math and Science Teacher

I love mentoring and working with children, learning new techniques to enhance my skills as an educator, dancing, exploring the outdoors, exercising, and traveling.

In Yolo County, my community service has been helping with the Mexican American Concilio. In Sacramento, my roll as an educator has been helping impact the youth.

My experience with Youth-On-The-Move was last year when I volunteered to help with the 32nd anniversary held at UC Davis.

The best memory from this event was being so encouraged to pursue my goals as a young educator and meeting so many professionals that have lots of knowledge and experience for me to learn from.

Julia Powers and grandson Le'Jon

Edmond Family

Joined Youth-on-the-Move, Inc. 1987

Mother: Julia Powers (age 63) One of YOMI's Families

Rebecca "Becky" Edmond – 10 years old when she joined YOMI, today (33 years later) she is 39 years old, she works in "In-Home Support;

Becky has three children – (1) Le'Jon, age 22; just graduated from Spartan College in Tulsa, OK and works at the Tulsa Airport in the aeronautical department

(2) Kierra, age 16 attends Sheldon High School, in Elk Grove, CA

(3) Kendric, age 12; attends T.R. Smedburg Middle School

Allen Wickham – 9 years old when he joined YOMI in 1987, today he is 39, works for Sacramento Transit Authority for 13 years

Miguel Perez & Linda Jaeckels, DTM

a YOMI member and mentor

My name is Miguel Perez. I was born in Fullerton, California at St. Jude Hospital, on August 1, 1991; I am 25 years old.

Currently, I work at First American Title Solutions located in Orange County, and I attend Fullerton Junior College in Fullerton, CA. majoring in Business Management. My hobbies are playing drums, hanging out with friends, exercising and jogging.

I've been involved with Youth-on-the-Move, Inc. (YOMI) for over five years. I have the privilege of working alongside of Dr. Pat and we serve our community and other surrounding communities. YOMI can continue to improve by serving local needs of the community and partnering with others to build a stronger community of support and love. I am also a role model and mentor in the program.

The Solomon Family

The West Family, Cornell, Cliff, and Mother, Irene

Countries Represented 2018 Hall of Fame

United States of America

Ukraine

Jamaica

Mexico

Argentina

India

Romania

Acjachemen Nation

EDUCATORS' HALL OF FAME
THE ALUMNI ASSOCIATION
of the YOUTH-ON-THE-MOVE, INC.
INTERNATIONAL EDUCATORS' HALL OF FAME

Mission Statement

The Alumni Association of the Youth-on-the-Move, Inc. International Educator's Hall of Fame serves:

1. to maintain and support the Educators' Hall of Fame;
2. to support, network with, and be role models and mentors for Youth-on-the-Move, Inc. and others;
3. to ensure recognition and to promote the legacies of outstanding multicultural educators in diverse academic disciplines for now and centuries to come.

FOUNDATION MEMBERS 10/95

Ida Dunson, '94
Ila Warner, '95
Sarah H. Hutchinson, '95
Dr. Paul Gulyassy, '95
Vikki Walker, '95
Frank Waller, '93
Dr. Patricia Adelekan, '97

ACTIVE MEMBERS

Ida Dunson, '94
Carolyn Stokes, '99
Dr. William H. Lee, '98
Gerald Bryant, '13
Dr. David Watkins '13
Rick Gonzales, '13
Frank Withrow, '97
Michael Benjamin, '13
Travis Parker, Jr. '13
Willie Portis, '13
Alan Rowe, '13
Lucia Birnbaum, '96
Al Jenkins, '96
Estaban Villa, '97
Al Wilson, '13
Joe Stinson, '13
Dr. Patricia Adelekan, '97
Linda Jaeckels, '13
Dr. Versie Burns, '14
Ollie Whitaker, '14
Dr. Lawrence B. de Graaf, '14
Jesse F. Berry, '14
Professor Ernest Bridges, '14

Sal Tinajero, '14
Louise Darling Whitaker, '14
Barbara Junious, '14
Robert (Bob) Johnson, '14
Dr. Kogee Thomas, '14
Bishop Franklin J. Harris, '15
Dr. DeVera H. Heard, '15
Lt. Colonel Alexander Jefferson, '15
Richard T. "Rick" Martinez, '15
Harry G. Oliver, '15
Caralyn Bell Percy, '15
Dr. Essie French Preston, '15
Ms. Frances M. Rios, '15
Rev. Linda Smith, '15
J Ramon Villanueva, '15
Margaret Ware, '15
The Iberall Family, '15
The Gonzalo Mendez Family, '15
The William Guzman Family, '15
R.Y.T.M.O. (Reaching Youth Through Music Opportunities), '15
Mike Anderson, '16
Mary Adams, '16

Nathan K. Banda '16
Harry L. Hoffebert, '16
Mrs. Sandy Lynn,'16 Holman, M.S.,'16
Dr. Carol Mattson,'16
Carlynn Lee McCormick,'16
Cynthia Michalak,'16
Justice Cruz Reynoso,'16
Patricia Ann Rucker, 16
Ms. Melrose Rowe,'16
Debra Jean McCoy Sorensen, M.S., '16
Anji Reddy Nalamalapu, '16

In Memoriam

Dr. Lorraine Boykin, ('95 -2017)
Neil Hollander, ('97 -2016)
Dr. Valarie Omega Justiss Vance, (1913-2015), '15
Mr. L. Ron Hubbard, (1911-1986), '15
Louis Alex Preston, Sr. (1935-2010), '15
John Favors, Jr. '93
Barbara Lawrence Hill, '14

Youth-on-the-Move
International Educators' Hall of Fame (IEHOF)
Legacy Museum and Learning Center

Purpose:
To help create and/or preserve (now and in the future) legacies of Inductees into the IEHOF – in positive and supportive learning environments.

Mission:
To highlight and preserve the achievements of great educators (past, present and future) who positively impact(ed) lives the world over and to engage inductees in positive intergenerational teaching and learning opportunities for youths, families and communities alike.

Vision:
To establish small museums located throughout communities – the world over – where people can visit, research and study the lives and contributions of outstanding achievers and history-makers in the field of education. To help youth succeed in life with the knowledge and help of these positive community role models. To help close the "Achievement Gap." The Hall of Famers are often "firsts," "founders," "pioneers," "trailblazers," and "movers-and-shakers" representing a plethora of disciplines/fields of knowledge. To engage in activities that will generate funds to help financially sustain the upkeep of the IEHOFLegacy Museum/learning center.

Location:
1850 E. 17th Street, #103, Santa Ana, CA 92705 – near public transportation, schools, churches, strip/shopping malls, houses, business districts, neighborhoods, office building, etc.

Components, activities of the Legacy Museums/learning centers (multi-purpose facilities, etc.):
1. Reading space – for reading and research.
2. Library/archives- to gather books, magazines, etc. about educators and their contributions
3. Space for classes, meetings, trainings, other gatherings
4. Analogue and digital image making (darkroom for photo development)
5. Computers, printers, scanners
6. Archives- of documents and other memorabilia
7. Showcases, other exhibit spaces
8. Book store, boutique, gallery to display and sell merchandise, art, etc.
9. Lounge for informal gatherings, resting, reading
10. Restrooms, kitchen/food preparation space,
11. Tables, chairs, couch(es)

How financed:
Memberships, admissions, grants, donations, fundraisers, bequeaths, charitable giving.
Money-generating activities: Bookstore, boutique, gallery: sell of items (books, t-shirts, stationary, candy, post cards, photos, etc) Auctions, Art shows, historical items, The Hall of Fame Events, and other valuables donated or created by members and donors.

Foundation Charter Members: Linda Jaeckels; Ollie Whittaker; Dr. Patricia Adelekan; Dr. Versie Burns; Rick Gonzales.

Museum 1P 5/2015 paa

Board of Directors

Dr. Patricia Adelekan
Founder/President, Hall Of Fame '95

Dr. Kogee Thomas
Hall Of Fame '14

Dr. David Watkins
Hall Of Fame '13

Brian Chuchua
Retired Businessman

Al Wilson
President, Folsom Zinfandel LLC

Dr. Versie Burns
Hall Of Fame '14

H.A. Rodrigo
President, ACO Sourcing Intl

Mahender Adluri
IT Manager

Hall of Fame Committee 2018

Maricruz Quezada
Student

Samuel Vance
Public Relations

Rick Gonzales
Retired Principal, Hall of Fame '13

James Burnell
Minister

Sharon Brandon
Youth

Barbara Gleason
Network

Rick Warren
Owner, RW Media

Florence Wariire
Youth Volunteer,
Slavic Missionary Church

"The Hall of Famers are very important...important to the past, to the present, and to the future. They have changed the world and will keep growing to make the world a better place. It is important for them to connect with each other and work within their different communities to bring attention and enlightenment about the Youth on the Move International Educators' Hall of Fame. Thanks to Dr. Patricia Adelekan for establishing the Hall of Fame around the world and empowering youth to succeed in school, the work world, and life in general."

– Dr. Kogee Thomas, '14

Order Additional Copies of International Educators' Hall of Fame Book

Your Name: _____

Shipping address: _____

City: _____ State: _____ Zip: _____

Email: _____

Year	Quantity	Price
2014	x $19.95 each	
2015	x $19.95 each	
2016	x $34.95 each	
2017	x $34.95 each	
2018 25th Anniversary	x $44.95 each	
Shipping:		
Total:		

Shipping: $3.50 for first book, each additional book add $1.50 each

Make check or Money Order payable to:
Adelekan Publishing Company
P.O. Box 5983 Garden Grove, CA 92846

For more information, go to www.EducatorsHallOfFame.org or call (714) 628-9844. All years available since 1993 - just ask!

Hello Members and Friends, We are trying to raise money to sponsor some youth to attend the event:

Cost to sponsor is $50.00 a youth. We have started already, won't you sponsor. We have 50 youths that need sponsoring. Thanks. Please let me know. Dr. Pat

This will pay for two meals and a program booklet. Please send me a note and let me know, you can also pay on line at Eventbrite or our website educatorshalloffame.org. If you know of a youth who may need a sponsor, please contact me. 714-628-9844

Youth Sponsors for 2018 – Plan now to sponsor youths for 2019!

Woment Civic Improvement Center - 10 • Dr. Patricia Adelekan -2 • Pastor James Burnell - 1

Mitch Minert - 2 • Mahender Adluri - 2 • Dr. Kogee Thomas -2WCIC (10)

Educators' Hall of Fame Nomination Form

To be eligible for nomination – all candidates must meet the following criteria

    (1) Be Retired from or

    (2) Have served for at least 20 years in the field of education (or a related field), and

    (3) Have done MORE than the CALL OF DUTY

CANDIDATE'S NAME _____

ADDRESS _____ STATE _____

PHONE _____ FAX _____

EMAIL _____ WEBSITE _____

(Nominations to the Educators' Hall of Fame may include, but not be limited to educators of diverse backgrounds in any of the following education categories: Preschool, Elementary, Mid-High Schools, Vocational, College/University (all levels and fields): administration, the arts, business, counseling, health, law, law enforcement, librarians, martial arts, medicine, music, nutrition, religion, support staff, etc.)

In FIFTY (50) WORDS OR LESS describe why you feel this person should be inducted into the Youth-on-the-Move Education International Educators' Hall of Fame.

_____
_____
_____
_____
_____
_____
_____

ATTACH TWO COPIES OF SUPPORTING DOCUMENTATION (IF AVAILABLE)

Nominator(s) Name(s) _____ Phone _____

Affiliation _____ Fax _____

Address _____ City _____ State _____

Email Address: _____ Website _____

Submit to:

iehof2015@gmail.com (subject line: IEHOF) or send to

IEHOF, P.O. Box 5983 Garden Grove, Ca. 92846, USA

714-628-9844

www.EducatorsHallOfFame.org

JACQUE SHERRILL TAHUKA-NUNEZ YOU HAVE MADE YOUR FATHER SO PROUD! CONGRATULATIONS! YOU HAVE TOUCHED THE HEARTS OF SO MANY, AND THE WORLD IS A BETTER PLACE BECAUSE OF YOU!
LOVE YOUR, DAD

JOURNEYSTOTHEPAST.COM (949) 248-2558

APPLIED SCHOLASTICS *Online* ACADEMY

Acknowledges Youth-on-the-Move

International Educators' Hall of Fame

25th Anniversary Jubilee

Our vision is to help create a world free from illiteracy by offering at home and online services where the uniqueness of the individual is embraced. The Applied Scholastics *Online* Academy, a non-profit organization dedicated to helping students acquire a lifelong love of learning, delivers K-12 curriculum and oversight services and is fully accredited by the Western Association of Schools and Colleges.

http://www.appliedscholasticsonline.com

Contact (951) 789-0224   registrar@appliedscholasticsonline.com

© 2018 Applied Scholastics *Online* Academy. All rights reserved. Applied Scholastics *Online* Academy is a non-profit, tax-exempt corporation and admits students of any race, religion, color, nationality or ethnic origin and is licensed to use Applied Scholastics™ educational services. Applied Scholastics and the Applied Scholastics open book design are trademarks and service marks owned by Association for Better Living and Education International and are used with its permission

---

3 Minute Vehicle Registration Services

Our services are geared towards Auto Dealers and the General Public who can't afford to spend extra time at the DMV. We are contracted, licensed and bonded by the state of California Department of Motor Vehicles, through the DMV business partner automated program (BPA) (Lic. #92334)

What we do:

- Yearly Vehicle Registration Renewals
- Replace Missing Stickers, License Plates or Vehicle Registration Cards
- Replace Lost or Missing Titles
- Transfer Ownership
- Duplicate Titles • Vehicle Verification
- License Plate or VIN Look-Up
- Out of State Transfers

All DMV registration renewal fees are also processed in real time, so if you're running late and don't have a lot of time to spend waiting in line, we are here for you.

Let us help make your DMV Registration Renewal simple.

WE ARE HERE TO SERVE YOU!

Kevin R. Gibbs
2326 Fulton Ave, Sacramento CA 95821
(916) 549-8318

From the entire

WCIC/Playmate Head Start Programs Family,

Congratulations

Edenausegboye B. P. Davis

for your

2018 Silver Jubilee Induction

Into The International Educators'

Hall of Fame!!!

WCIC, Non-Profit 501(c) 3
edavis@dons.usfca.edu
Ms. Davis

THE OK PROGRAM

A 501 (C)(3) NONPROFIT YOUTH ORGANIZATION

CONGRATULATES ALL OF THE 2018 INDUCTEES

INTO THE INTERNATIONAL EDUCATORS' HALL OF FAME

ON ITS 25TH YEAR (SILVER JUBILEE) &

TO ALL THE YOUTH-ON-THE-MOVE, INC. ALUMNI

ON THEIR 33 YEAR ANNIVERSARY

RETIRED DEPUTY SHERRIFF FROM SACRAMENTO

DONALD NORTHCROSS

CEO, FOUNDER

OKPROGRAM.ORG

CURRENTLY OPERATING AT GRANT HIGH SCHOOL, SACRAMENTO

Order your copy of Dr. Pat's new book –
__A Teenager's Handbook for Success, Vol. 1__

Inspirational Quotes

To order, send $10 per book to:
Youth-on-the-Move, Inc.
1850 E. 17th Street, #103,
Santa Ana, CA 92705
or order online at
YouthOnTheMove.net

VRWebServices

Services
- Website Design
- Website Hosting
- Domain Registration
- E-commerce
- SEO
- Social Media Marketing

Von J. Roy - Senior Software Engineer
Email: von.roy@gmail.com
Website: vonroy.net
Phone: 714-292-4139

We will design, modify or uprade your website to the latest quality standards, using google analytics and search engine optimization principles to ensure your website can be found quickly in all major search engines by words and phrases relevant to what your site is offering.

We will ensure that your website has optimized page content (for speed, ease of use and accuracy) and that your website is responsive so that the design adapts to different browsers and the content is resized to fit all screens (smart phones, tablets, laptops as well as desktops).

We will monitor your website for potential security issues, addressing them quickly and efficiently.

Our goal is to provide you and your customers with a positive user experience!

"We stay ready so we don't have to get ready."

Wisdom of the Ages

By Patricia Adelekan, Ph.D., DTM x 2, CTA, January 2013, Anaheim, CA ; and revised, July 28, 2018 for the 25th Anniversary (Silver Jubilee) of the International Educators' Hall of Fame – to Preserve Legacies, Honor Excellence and to Unite Generations. I hereby share some of the principles which guide my life and hopefully might guide yours, too.

1. Know and Share Thyself.
2. Enter to Learn; go out to serve.
3. Patience and perseverance are two vital keys to success.
4. Forgiveness works patience and love.
5. Love is patience.
6. Challenge yourself to the number of acts of kindness you can do in a day.
7. The fruit of the spirit lead to peace and happiness.
8. The International Magna Carter: The Universal Declaration Human Rights are to lift man to a greater standard - Raise the level of human dignity. Rededicate our moral integrity.
9. A mantra to adopt and recite daily is the "fruit of the spirit."
10. Strike out with love and conviction at all injustice and violence.
11. What do you wish for all mankind?
12. Idle spectators are guilty, contributors to anarchy, uneasiness, problems, violence.
13. To live with dignity: one must practice faith, work, love, justice, fairness, gentleness, kindness, nonviolence, compassion.
14. Fundamental unity on all things depends on universal responsibility of our humanity coupled with positive and decisive action.
15. Say to yourself constantly, "I shall pass through this world but once. Any good, therefore, that I can do or any kindness that I can show to any fellow creature, let me do it now. Let me not defer nor neglect it, for I shall not pass this way again. By Etienne de Grelle
16. "There is only one way to happiness and that is to cease worrying about things which are beyond the power of our will." By Epictetus

An Array of Hero Preachers, Teachers & Students

Who are the true heroes of our society? High-priced athletes who dunk a basket ball? Multimillion dollar entertainers who make us laugh? Our society appears to place high value on sports and entertainment while neglecting to reward many who make critical contributions —including the people in whose hands we entrust our precious next generation.

Today's real heroes are the educators who every day face the problem of too many students in the classroom, too few books, too many kids and adults on drugs, and too many parents who don't seem to care. Many educators go above and beyond the call of duty every day. Month after month. Year after year.

Yet society under- appreciates and under-compensates them.
This needs to be corrected.

Let us all take a moment to thank and honor a few caring and outstanding Educators!
Let us today salute the real heroes of the world:

OUR EDUCATORS
Youth-on-the-Move, Inc.
INTERNATIONAL EDUCATORS' HALL OF FAME

SAN MANUEL BAND OF MISSION INDIANS

WARMLY CONGRATULATES

JACQUE NUNEZ

ON BEING INDUCTED INTO THE

2018 YOUTH-ON-THE-MOVE INTERNATIONAL EDUCATORS' HALL OF FAME

THANK YOU FOR YOUR SUPPORT AND DEDICATED SERVICE TO THE COMMUNITY.

sanmanuel-nsn.gov

Congratulations and God Bless

Youth-on-the-Move, Inc. and the International Educators Hall of Fame and Youth Awards

TBC BECOMING A 5-STAR CHURCH;
"I AM A CHURCH MEMBER"
OUR VISIONGRAM
WORSHIP
You were planned for God's pleasure
FELLOWSHIP
You were formed for God's family
DISCIPLESHIP
You were created to become like Christ
MINISTRY
You were shaped to serve God
EVANGELISM
You were made for a mission

VISION
INTEGRITY
STRUCTURE
ACCOUNTABILITY

PRAYER ~ BIBLE ~ STEWARDSHIP

SERVICE TIMES:
SUNDAY SCHOOL 9:30 - 10:30 AM

SUNDAY SERVICE 10:45 AM

PRAYER MEETING
WEDNESDAY 7:00 - 8:00 PM

The Reverend Dr. Tokunbo Adelekan and the Tabernacle Baptist Church Family
"We are God's children, reaching out to all people and equipping them to live more abundantly in Jesus Christ."

380 S. Broadway Street | Dayton, Ohio 45402
Office: (937) 228-6393 ~ Fax: (937) 228-5584
www.tabernacleofdayton.org

Thank you, Dr. Rose, for being a fearless leader and tireless advocate for higher education.

Congratulations on being inducted into the

2018 International Educators' Hall of Fame!

SANTA ANA COLLEGE

Congratulations!!!

Crowning Partners Corp

Costa Mesa & Newport Beach, CA

Corporate Finance

Mergers & acquisitions

Real Estate Transitions

Corporate Law

Gboyega Adelekan, Esq
310-864-9702

Founding Member of Youth-on-the-Move, Inc.

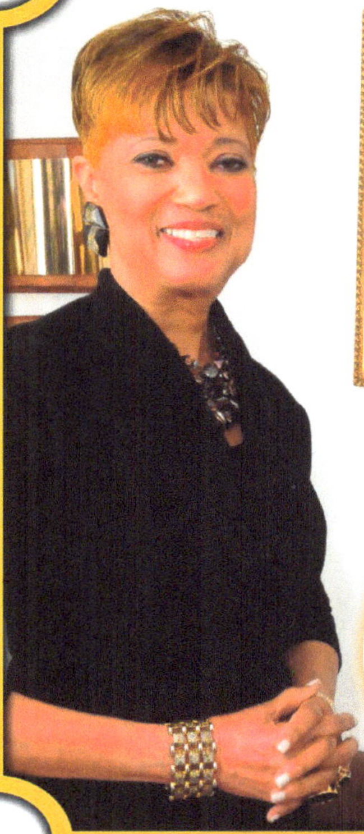

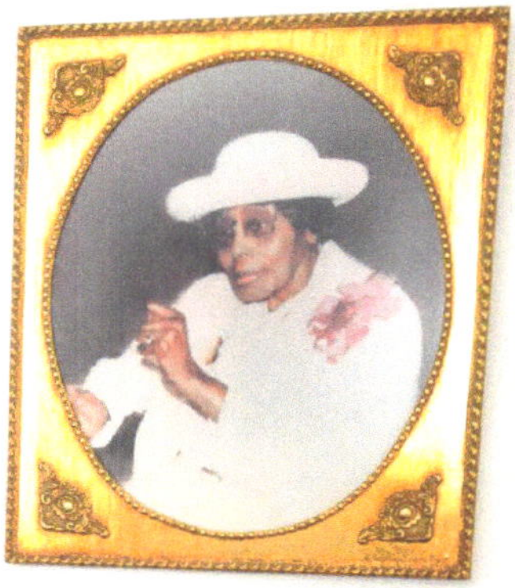

CANDID EXPRESSION
OF "MOM"
CAPTURED ON WOMEN'S DAY
NATIONAL CONVOCATION 1988
DR. MATTIE McGLOTHEN

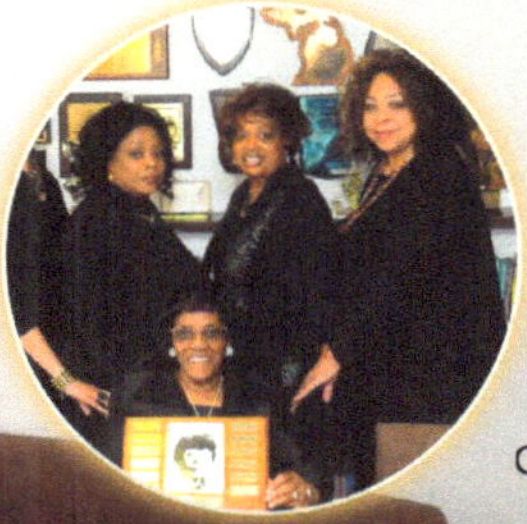

EXECUTIVE
BOARD
OF DIRECTORS

THE DR. EMMA J. CLARK FOUNDATION, INC. CONGRATULATES DORIS I. MANGRUM

FOR BEING INDUCTED INTO THE 2018 INTERNATIONAL EDUCATORS' HALL OF FAME

Dr. Emma J. Clark
Foundation, Inc.
LITERACY + HISTORY: DISCOVERING IMPORTANT LINKS

WWW.MCGLOTHENLIBRARYMUSEUM.ORG

The Jazz Institute of Chicago
is pleased to congratulate
Director of Education and Artist Development

Diane Chandler-Marshall, M.A.

on her 2018 induction into the
25th Anniversary Celebration
of the Youth-on-the-Move
International Educators' Hall of Fame

CHANGING LIVES THROUGH JAZZ

jazz institute of chicago

Founded in 1969, the Jazz Institute of Chicago promotes and nurtures jazz in Chicago by providing jazz education, developing and supporting musicians, building audiences and fostering a thriving jazz scene. Visit **jazzinchicago.org** to find out more!

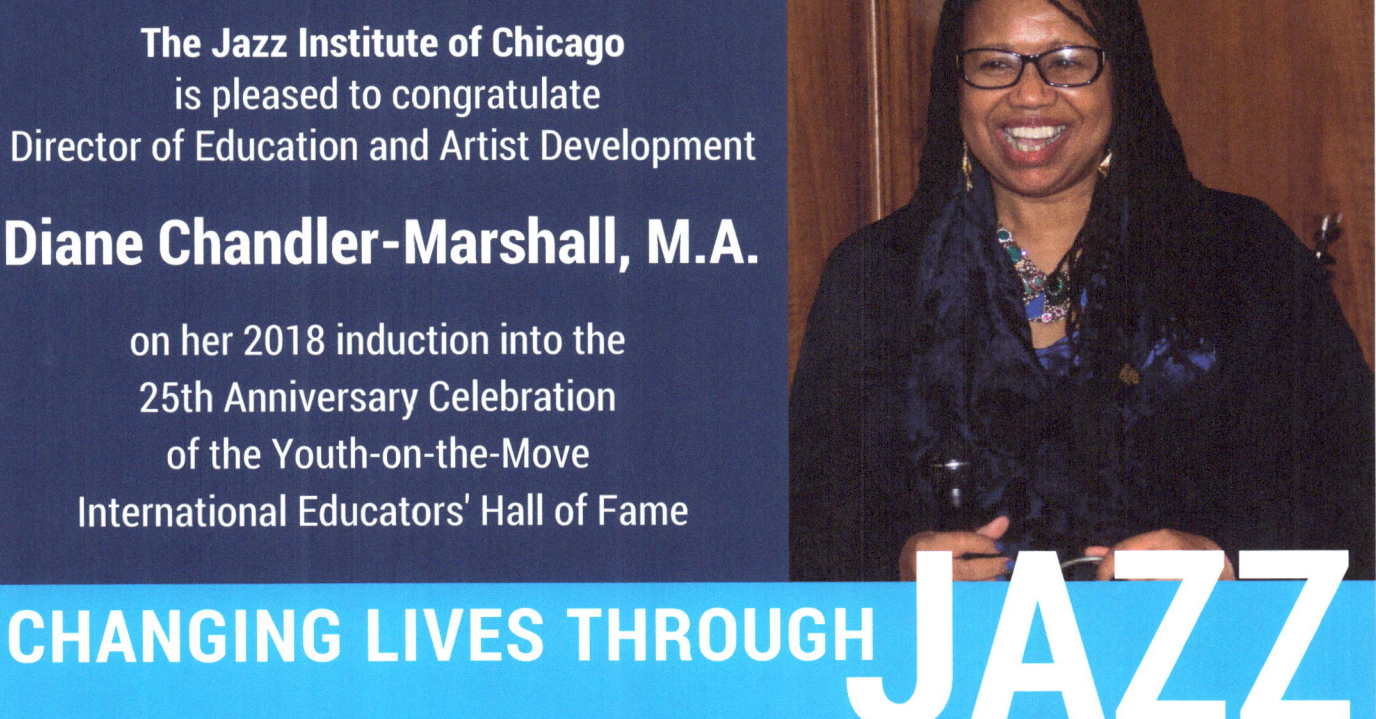

Clay Bock (714) 420-1911
Mary Ann Bock (714) 931-0111

Integrity Jewelers

Celebrating 30 Years Doing All Aspects of Fine Jewelry!

11088 Trask Ave. Suite 100 • Garden Grove, CA 92843
Clay: Integrity@earthlink.net • Mary Ann: mam50@earthlink.net

JAMES A BURNELL
Associate
jimburnell4911@hotmail.com

TALKFUSION
www.talkfusion.com/1456397
1-714-661-0763

Sister **Wanda Scott** "Golden Words"
AUTHOR OF "TAKE YOUR VISION OUT OF THE CLOSET"
714-988-5194
E-MAIL: wandascottprayers@yahoo.com

ESL Toastmasters Club No. 1

Meetings on 1st and 3rd Sunday's of each month
12:30 p.m. - 2:30- p.m

Grace Church of Orange, Trailer Room A2
2201 E. Fairhaven Ave., Orange, CA 92869

Guests are welcomed.

ESL.ToastmastersClubs.org
Email OFFICERS-1565170@ToastmastersClubs.org

Youth-on-the-Move
Enter to Learn:
Go out to service

Patricia Adelekan, Ph.D; DTM
Founder, CEO
www.YouthOnTheMove.net

Be a giver
All who give, get

Youth & Seniors
Training
Teaching
Mentoring

Program Evaluations
Research
501(C)(3) #68-0139194

English/ESL Experts
Accent Reduction
Speaking
Writing

(714) 628-9844

Congratulations

To the Newly Opened in 2015

*Educators' Legacy Museum
and
Learning Center*

1850 E. 17th Street, #103
Santa Ana CA 92705
(714) 628-9844

Linda Jaeckels, DTM
Founding Charter Member

www.ingramcontent.com/pod-product-compliance
Lightning Source LLC
Chambersburg PA
CBHW041440010526
44118CB00002B/134